The New Left and Christian Radicalism

The New Left and Christian Radicalism

by

ARTHUR G. GISH

WILLIAM B. EERDMANS PUBLISHING COMPANY
Grand Rapids, Michigan

To *Brethren Life and Thought* we gratefully acknowledge permission to reprint portions of Part I, which appeared in the Spring, 1969 issue.

To
PEGGY
and
DALE MARTIN

Preface

To be radical is to go to the root, to attack a problem at its base. To be radical is to present a fundamental alternative to the status quo. It means to start with what could be rather than what is.

This approach is characteristic both of the New Radicalism that is emerging in Western society and Christian Radicalism as found in the Left Wing of the Reformation. Part One of this book is a comparison of the New Left and sixteenth-century Anabaptism. The implication is that we are dealing here not with two isolated movements, but rather with what seems to be a pattern of the moving of the Spirit in history. Many other radical movements, such as the Franciscans or the Quakers, could have been used for this comparison. Throughout history there have always been radical alternatives to establishment thinking. Church historians often refer to this phenomenon as the "Free Church tradition."

Part Two of this study is an attempt to make a synthesis of New Left and Anabaptist thought by examining the current issues in theology, ethics, and politics from the radical perspective presented in Part One. After developing a biblical and theological basis for radicalism, the issues of compromise, revolution, civil disobedience, and related matters are dealt with directly.

This study is written both for the humanistic radical who has never seen the relevance of theology to social change, and for those Christians who have never realized the radical implications of the Christian faith. It is written in the belief that any movement needs a well-grounded philosophy to

7

guide it. While that philosophy should not be dogmatic, closed, or purely rationalistic, it can maintain an openness and still give direction and meaning to the events in which one participates.

This work would not have been possible without the stimulation and the challenging of my ideas by my friends, my teachers, and the Faw family. Special thanks must be given to Donald F. Durnbaugh and Dale W. Brown, who have given me so much help and inspiration. Thanks also to Carolyn Cassidente, who typed the manuscript. My deepest gratitude goes to my wife Peggy for her patience and love.

Credit also must be given to my parents and the West Greentree Church of the Brethren from whom I received most of these ideas in the first place. Perhaps my Sunday school teachers did not realize the radical implications of the biblical faith they imparted to me, but the message I received from them is greatly appreciated.

— ART GISH

Table of Contents

PART ONE

PART TWO

Part One

CHAPTER ONE

An Analysis of the New Left

> *There is nothing so powerful in all the*
> *world as an idea whose time has come.*
> Victor Hugo

Introduction

On February 17, 1966, Charles W. Engelhard, Jr., received
the Brotherhood Award from the National Conference of
Christians and Jews. Outside the hotel were about 350 pickets
protesting the meeting. Why? Because this "liberal," in addition to being a philanthropist, is also the director of two
dozen companies in South Africa, and sits on the commis-
sions that decide working conditions in South Africa and
draft native labor for his mines.[1] Most of the pickets were
"young radicals," members of what is called the New Left.
This incident illustrates both the crisis of American Liberalism and the mood of the New Left.

In contrast to the silent stupor of the fifties, the decade of
the sixties has been filled with activism, protest, and controversy. A new generation of youth not only has made itself
vocal, but has had a disturbing effect upon the establishment.
What important government or university official has not
felt compelled to try to dismiss the importance of the young

[1] *New Left Notes,* February 25, 1966, p. 1.

radicals who have created for them so many headaches? Out of the larger movement for peace and civil rights has come a new style of political activity, a loosely connected group commonly referred to as the New Left.

A definitive interpretation of this new phenomenon is impossible, since the movement is so loosely organized and still only in the process of emerging. Besides, this analysis is only one interpretation of what the New Left is essentially about. It is the vision this author received through his participation in the movement. Other radicals may disagree with this definition and perspective, but it is through these contrasting analyses that the New Left will continue to grow and evolve. Most of the focus of this chapter will be on Students for a Democratic Society (SDS), since this is the group the author knows best.

Many attempts have been made to define what the New Left is. One could include all dissenters on the left, from disenchanted liberals to hippies and dropouts. We will take a rather narrow definition of the New Left, however. A distinction is being made here between the political activist and the socially alienated.[2] Our main interest is in the political radicals, although the hippie movement and other forms of protest would fit much of our description. We are more concerned with activists than with those who would retreat into a "community of love," more interested in political protest than in the mystical world of drugs.

Organizationally, the New Left by our definition would encompass SDS, Student Nonviolent Coordinating Committee (SNCC), Southern Student Organizing Committee (SSOC), The Resistance, women's liberation groups, and numerous *ad hoc* committees. Although not all in these groups would fit our description of the New Left, these groups would be the center of the New Left movement.

A clear distinction must be made between the New Left and the Old Left. Among the groups in the Old Left are the Progressive Labor Party (PL), the Communist Party, and

---

[2] Kenneth Keniston, "The Sources of Student Dissent," *Journal of Social Issues,* XXIII (July, 1967), pp. 110-116.

the various Trotskyite sects. However, it must be noted that during 1968-69, SNCC and SDS hardly fit the definition of the New Left as described in this chapter. It would be our contention that during this period these groups moved out of the New Left orbit and reverted to an Old Left stance. Our narrow definition of the New Left is somewhat of an "ideal type," but one that does fit SDS and other groups from 1961 until at least 1967. It may also be that SDS will again move to a more New Left position since there are still many New Left people in SDS. No attempt is made to evaluate the Black Panther Party.

Included in this description of the New Left are those who were in the Freedom Rides in the South, who in the early sixties demonstrated against the House Committee on Un-American Activities (HUAC), who pleaded for the life of condemned Caryl Chessman, who picketed for the Test Ban Treaty, who participated in Mississippi Summer, who led the Free Speech Movement, and who have organized resistance to the draft and the Vietnam war. They are now helping striking farm workers in the San Joaquin Valley of California, organizing the poor in the slum communities of the North and Appalachia, and organizing for freedom within the universities. They are a generation that has been disillusioned with America, yet optimistic about the changes that can be brought about. They are dedicated to "changing the system."

This study aims primarily to analyze the underlying ideology of the New Left rather than its history or its political and economic philosophy. Although many references will be made to these latter areas, the main concern is to examine the values, goals, and implicit theology of the young radicals. Extensive quotations have been included to give the reader a flavor of their writing and temperament.

Historical Background

In 1959, Sidney Lens wrote that "one of the striking features of American postwar life has been the virtual disappearance of the American Left."[3] There was a missing generation of American leftists. Lens saw the problem as a "mass man mentality" with conformity as its rule. The fifties were a time of turning inward toward oneself and away from the larger world. A case in point is the strong emphasis on psychology as the great witch doctor during this time. Because of the repressive nature of McCarthyism, the decline of the Old Left partly due to inner dissension and the revelations of Stalinism, and the dullness of the Eisenhower administration, students were discouraged from any radical activity and were even afraid to sign petitions because "it might hurt you later on." On many campuses the most radical act was the annual panty raid. It is interesting to note that a mere ten years ago students were admonished by adults to show concern about the urgent issues of the day and to dare to be different. Today students are warned by their elders about the dangers of irresponsible protest.

However, by the end of the fifties a new era was beginning to dawn. The Beat Generation sensed that there was something wrong with our society. They were disillusioned and angry, but lacked the vision to do anything but withdraw from society. The Civil Rights Movement had begun to develop through the success of the nonviolent direct-action tactics of Martin Luther King, Jr. People began to see hope for changing society. The early New Left radicals were impressed with the vision of pacifist A. J. Muste and his vigorous opposition to militarism and the Cold War. They identified with the Zengakuren students who kept Eisenhower from visiting Japan by their snake-dance demonstrations. They were also influenced by the pacifist and socialist British New Left, which arose in the late fifties and published the *New Left Review*. At the University of Wisconsin left-wing students, through the influence of Professor William Appleman Williams, in 1959 began publishing *Studies on the Left*, an important theoretical journal for New Left intellectuals. The movement had begun.

---

[3] Sidney Lens, "The Mass Man," *The Progressive*, XXIII (January, 1959), p. 15.

The election of President John F. Kennedy in 1960 had a significant impact on American youth. There was a new openness to criticism and renewal. Suddenly social change seemed possible. Commitment became feasible. Youth responded to Kennedy's proclamation that "the torch has been passed to a new generation of Americans." Even though radicals now call Kennedy a phony liberal and reject both his foreign and domestic policies, it cannot be denied that he challenged them, made politics once more respectable, and gave them a vision of change.

The New Left probably was born with the first student lunch-counter sit-in at Greensboro, North Carolina, on February 11, 1960, and the founding of SNCC in April of that year. A movement had started that would form the embryo of the New Left. White students from the North began going South to work with SNCC. It was largely through the inspiration of SNCC that SDS developed. SDS officially got started at its founding convention, June 11-15, 1962, in Port Huron, Michigan. Out of this conference came the famous founding statement of SDS, *The Port Huron Statement*. Among those founders were Tom Hayden and Paul Potter, both who were beaten in McComb, Mississippi in October 1961. It was in SNCC that the basic ideals of SDS were found. As Carl Oglesby, past president of SDS, put it, "At our best, I think we are SNCC translated to the North.... Our best concern comes from SNCC."[4] In 1963 SDS people formed the Economic Research and Action Project (ERAP), which began organizing projects in Northern cities, the most famous being in Newark and JOIN in Chicago. On April 17, 1965, SDS organized the first major march on Washington against the Vietnam war. In spite of strong opposition from the liberal community, twenty thousand marchers participated. From that time on, SDS has been seen as an important antiwar group. It soon became the largest and most active radical student group.

---

[4] Quoted by Jack Newfield, *Prophetic Minority* (New York: Signet Books, 1966), p. 90.

Motivating Factors

The basis for the New Left cannot be found in any great book or any prophet. In fact, there is no simple explanation of their motivation. Their background is neither Marx, Trotsky, nor Mao, but more correctly Albert Camus, Bob Dylan, and Paul Goodman. The Civil Rights Movement was very important. But still more basic is their personal experience. They have experienced the evils they deplore. Their reactions are based more on gut-level right-and-wrong feelings than on any social theory. Casey Hayden, a SNCC worker, describes this experience.

> I've read about some of these ideas in articles about the New Left and they always sound very mystical. They're not, at least for me. They are rooted in experiences of organizing and are very concrete. They are the base for whatever ideas I have about how society could function more humanely.[5]

Although it has had a significant impact, Marxism cannot be used to explain their longing for social and economic justice or their antiestablishment behavior. In fact, many have never read Marx. The New Left is actually an interesting mixture of socialism, anarchism, and pacifism.

They are children of the affluent society, and have made what Richard Flacks has called "a revolt of the advantaged."[6] They were reared in an atmosphere of security and unequaled opportunity, and were given everything they could ask for. They knew there was a place for them in society, but that place had little meaning for them. A comfortable job and status were not really what they were looking for. These were unable to provide answers to the deepest problems of life. They became aware of a spiritual poverty in our society, aware that work and success are not the only measure of meaning.

They grew up in the late forties and fifties and were raised in democratic homes. They are the children of Dr.

---

[5] Casey Hayden, "Raising the Question of Who Decides," *Thoughts of the Young Radicals* (A New Republic Book, 1966), p. 47.

[6] Richard Flacks, "The Liberated Generation: Roots of Student Protest," *Journal of Social Issues*, XXIII (July, 1967), p. 55.

Spock. In this democratic setting they felt free to challenge
the authority of their parents, and often succeeded. When
they met the larger society they also expected rationality and
consensus. They were unprepared for the authoritarian structures they were to meet.

But even more significantly, they were reared in the best
tradition of the American heritage. To grasp their movement
correctly, one must understand that it is basically an American spirit. They have taken America's ideals seriously. The
things they are saying have been the usual diet of graduation
speeches. The difference with them is that they believe those
ideals and take them seriously. As Michael Harrington put it,

> They seemed to have believed what they were told about free-
> dom, equality, justice, world peace and the like. They became
> activists in order to affirm these traditional values with regard to
> some ethical cause. . . .[7]

They believed the proclamation that this was a "nation con-
ceived in liberty and dedicated to the proposition that all
men are created equal." But when they looked around, they
saw that reality was much different from the myths they
were taught. When they learned of discrimination, exploitation, and militarism, they were morally repulsed. This is the
heart of their revolt. Their break with the establishment is
not because they are anti-American, but because they think
the establishment is. They felt deceived by a society that
talked in platitudes and published impressive statistics proving its accomplishments, but was incapable of solving the
urgent problems of civil rights, poverty, and foreign policy.
They came to see American society as dishonest and hypocritical.[8] The gap between America's ideals and her actions
was too great. Carl Oglesby at the November 27, 1965 march
on Washington declared,

---

[7] Michael Harrington, "The Mystical Militants," *Thoughts of the
Young Radicals* (A New Republic Book, 1966), p. 66.

[8] I can well remember the emotional crisis I experienced during the
Bay of Pigs invasion. I had been coming to more and more distrust of
my government. This straw broke the camel's back. The U.S. government was no longer to be trusted. I too was on my way to radicalism.

> . . . Others will make of it that I sound mighty anti-American. To these I say: Don't blame *me* for *that!* Blame those who mouthed my liberal values and broke my American heart.[9]

Their rebellion began with very basic, concrete issues. They simply believed that Negroes should be treated with justice, that preparation for nuclear war should be stopped, that people should have the opportunity for a good life. Economic and political analyses came later. Because of these moderate goals, they began going to the South to help people register to vote. In the South they realized how naive they had been. There they went through a process of radicalization.

These are the people who watched Black people stand in line to register to vote, only to be turned away. They saw civil rights workers beaten by police because they wanted to take sandwiches to those standing in line. They witnessed the firehoses, the police dogs, and the cattle prodders. They experienced the Southern jails. They tried to change the system, but the system would not change. They had faced the power of the establishment and were forced to change their attitudes toward that establishment. They learned that the more one tries to change things, the more he realizes how entrenched the problem is. Soon what was originally an ethical revolt began to take on political and economic content.

Staughton Lynd tells of Bob Moses, who had put so much of himself into voter registration, going to Africa and seeing a magazine published by the United States Information Agency. There was a picture with Bob Moses and Fannie Lou Hamer with the caption: "Bob Moses and Mrs. Hamer leading delegates of the Mississippi Freedom Democratic Party to their seats at the Democratic Party Convention." Bob knew that the government was lying and using him to project an image of freedom around the world. As Lynd puts it, "Robert Moses, gentlest of men, returned to the United States convinced that no infamy or perfidy was beyond the capacities of this country."[10]

---

[9] Carl Oglesby, *Let Us Shape the Future* (Chicago: Students for a Democratic Society), p. 5.

[10] Staughton Lynd, "A Radical Speaks in Defense of S.N.C.C.," *New York Times Magazine,* September 10, 1967, Section 6, p. 152.

The discontent of the New Left was also fed on the university campus. At first the issue was civil rights. There was little interest in university reform until the university began to get in the way of civil rights activities. Then some students began to see how the university was also a part of the "corporate structure." As Steve Weissman, a Berkeley student, put it,

> In 1964 we didn't much care, at first, how they were running Berkeley. We were trying to collect money for going South and for working in the Oakland ghetto. All of a sudden the university administration began making it tough. That's how the campus demonstrations started.[11]

In the university they found the same bureaucracy, the same lack of freedom that exists in the rest of society. Students felt like an alien group within the multiversity. As there was more and more emphasis upon research, status, and bureaucratic complexity, the students have become more and more alienated. One observer put it as follows:

> Today's university campus has become for many students the last point in their lives in which they see any hope for exercising significant influence. The activist youth have seen the bureaucratized world make older voices whisper thin. The campus seems the last stronghold for testing ways of influencing their world. They are afraid that when they leave the university, get a job, marry and raise a family, the weight of responsibility will weaken their impetus for change. Those over thirty are not to be trusted, because of their increasing investment in the system as it exists.[12]

Who are these students? From a nationwide study, summarized by Joseph Katz of Stanford University, Dr. Katz concluded that "activists as a group are more intelligent, less prejudiced and psychologically more stable than nonactivists."[13] In various studies (Heist, 1965; Somers, 1965) psychological tests have shown them to be exceptionally high in flexibility, intelligence, objectivity, independence, and sensi-

---

[11] Quoted by Harvey Wasserman, "Reform, Not Revolution," *The Progressive*, XXXI (August, 1967), p. 27.

[12] Edward E. Sampson, "Student Activism and the Decade of Protest," *Journal of Social Issues*, XXIII (July, 1967), p. 21.

[13] *New York Times*, June 19, 1967, p. 29.

tivity.[14] Keniston concludes that "... the higher the student's grade average, the more outstanding his academic achievements, the more likely it is that he will become involved in any given political demonstration."[15]

This could be called the sensitive generation. They know what is happening in the world and are quick to perceive any injustice or deception. They need not be given a discourse on why the government is wrong about Vietnam. All they need to do is listen to official pronouncements in order to be turned off. They claim to have seen through what they consider administration jargon and double-talk. They feel they know when someone isn't "telling it like it is."

They are motivated also by the realization that they may be the last generation to have the opportunity to work for freedom. They have understood the growing totalitarianism of our technological, centralized society. Theirs is the existentialist revolt against the dehumanization of our modern world, the transformation of man into an object. It is the search for authenticity in the midst of depersonalization and objectification. They are asking whether technology and bureaucracy can be mastered and put to the use of man, or whether we are doomed to a technocratic totalitarianism. But there is also the bomb. Therefore, in the early sixties they worked for nuclear disarmament, channeling much of their effort through the Student Peace Union (SPU). They understood the folly of war and were not going to be brainwashed by any slogans such as "The war to end all wars," or "To make the world safe for democracy." They would rather work to make democracy safe for the world.

No one knows where the movement would be apart from the Vietnam war. This was the event that completely turned the activists against the system. The moral indignation raised

---

[14] James W. Trent and Judith L. Craise, "Commitment and Conformity in the American College," *Journal of Social Issues*, XXIII (July, 1967), pp. 38-41. This entire issue deals with sociological and psychological studies of the protest generation and with this question in particular.

[15] Keniston, p. 117.

by the systematic destruction of a small nation fed large numbers of people into the movement. Antiwar marches and teach-ins became the platform for the New Left to reach those who were still uninvolved. Much of the size and activity of the New Left must be related to this war. The war continues to raise the question about the kind of society in which we live. The New Left is helping to sharpen these questions.

The New Left Analysis of Society

Protest led to a more systematic analysis of our society. Radicals concluded that the problem was not merely a few imperfections, but rather that society is sick to the core. Their analysis soon included all of American life. They recognized that they must go beyond their gut-level reaction to society to make a radical analysis of that society. Their analysis stands in contrast to the respected views of men like Daniel Bell, Talcott Parsons, Arthur Schlesinger, Jr., Seymour Lipset, and others. They are much closer to C. Wright Mills, Paul Goodman, and Herbert Marcuse.

They recognized that their analysis had to be radical. As they worked on reforms, they realized that to begin to put dignity and equality into the lives of the disinherited would mean thoroughgoing rearrangements in our system. But they soon learned that their questions were not being taken seriously. In the *Port Huron Statement,* this indictment was made:

> The questions we might want raised — what is really important? can we live in a different and better way? if we wanted to change society, how would we do it? — are not thought to be questions of a "fruitful, empirical nature," and thus are brushed aside.[16]

They wanted to ask how society could be changed to allow more freedom and responsibility. But they learned that these questions were not acceptable.

> We must be careful not to speak too passionately about freedom, justice, love, peace, or happiness. For (and we've been warned)

---

[16] *The Port Huron Statement* (Chicago: Students for a Democratic Society, 1962), p. 5.

"Love and peace are nice, but you're not very realistic; you're kind of offbeat."[17]

Soon they realized that the problem is not injustice, poverty, racial discrimination, or any of the other evils they were protesting. Vietnam is not the problem. It is not the reason for our failure to come to grips with poverty, dying cities, and education. Rather Vietnam is a manifestation of our problem. The problem is the system. The issue is not Birchite generals or Southern rednecks, but a "managed society" controlled by respectable men-liberals. Tom Hayden explains,

> My own disenchantment with the U.S. didn't really come because of its failures in Negro rights and foreign policy, but with the realization . . . that responsibility for these things lies with the most respectable people in society . . . people in the North with connections with the foundations, corporations and banks and the Democratic Party, who parade in their own suburban communities as liberals, but who happen to own, lock, stock, and barrel, the major enterprises in Mississippi.[18]

In another article Hayden puts it even more strongly: ". . . Then disenchantment really begins: with the understanding that the most respected and enlightened Americans are among the most barbarous."[19] In reference to Vietnam, Oglesby pointed out at the November 27, 1965 march on Washington,

> Think of the men who engineer that war — those who study the maps, give the commands, push the buttons, and tally the dead; Bundy, McNamara, Rusk, Lodge, Goldberg, the President himself. They are not moral monsters. They are all honorable men. They are all liberals.[20]

Paul Potter, in his speech at the April 17, 1965 march on Washington, said that we must name the system that controls us, analyze it, and finally change it. He asked,

> What kind of system is it that justifies the United States or any country seizing the destinies of the Vietnamese people and using

---

[17] Bill Ayers, "A Community for Kids," *New Left Notes*, June 26, 1967, p. 24.

[18] Quoted by Paul Jacobs and Saul Landau, *The New Radicals* (New York: Vintage Books, 1966), p. 34.

[19] Tom Hayden, "The Politics of 'The Movement,'" *Dissent*, XIII (January-February, 1966), p. 75.

[20] Oglesby, p. 2.

them callously for its own purpose? What kind of system is it that disenfranchises people in the South, leaves millions upon millions of people throughout the country impoverished and excluded from the mainstream and promise of American society, that creates faceless and terrible bureaucracies and makes those the place where people spend their lives and do their work, that consistently puts material values before human values — and still persists in calling itself free and still persists in finding itself fit to police the world? What place is there for ordinary men in that system and how are they to control it, make it bend itself to their wills rather than bending them to its?[21]

They named the system "Corporate Liberalism." It is a system that extends from the Cold War to Welfare, from liberal investment in South Africa to the bureaucratic control of the university. It is the organization of society according to the large corporation model, controlled by a small elite (C. Wright Mills). It is a system that excludes people from making decisions that affect their own lives. It is the military-industrial complex, which profits from the continuation of the Cold War and military actions in underdeveloped countries. Thus the New Left sees the government of this country as doing bad things, but more importantly it sees that the government represents and is controlled by the people who benefit from those bad things. For example, in 1954 the democratically elected president of Guatemala was overthrown by a C.I.A.-supported coup. Before this, he had attempted to nationalize a portion of United Fruit Company's plantations for land reform. The next year, Gen. Walter Bedell Smith, who was director of the C.I.A. in 1954, joined the board of directors of the United Fruit Company. Or in 1965 in the Dominican Republic, our "neutral" peacemaker was Ellsworth Bunker, Jr., a board member and stockholder in the National Sugar Refining Company, a corporation with major interests in the Dominican Republic.[22] New Left people have done much research into this sort of thing and found that the decisions of basic policy are often made by people with vested interests in those decisions.

The system is called corporatism because of the power of

---

[21] New York: Students for a Democratic Society, 1965.
[22] Oglesby, p. 7.

the major corporations to shape decisions and structure society after their own models. It is liberalism because the system has taken on both the personnel and the rhetoric of liberalism in order to achieve its ends, the accumulation of more and more goods and power for a small percentage of the world's population. The New Left sees the United States as not being concerned with the freedom of people around the world, but caring about markets and trade. The important thing about Guatemala is the United Fruit Company. This then is seen as the reason we support dictators like Diem and Franco, and try to destroy Castro.

For the New Left, the problem is not man, but an evil system that forces men to do evil deeds. Acting as individuals, they would be unable to commit the same acts. Probably even Johnson would be unable to burn a child with napalm, yet he has done it to thousands of children. Oglesby, in the above-mentioned speech, stated,

> We do not say these men are evil. We say, rather, that good men can be divided from their compassion, by the institutional system that inherits us all. Generation in and out, we are put to use. People become instruments. Generals do not hear the screams of the bombed; sugar executives do not see the misery of the cane cutters: for to do so is to be that much *less* the general, that much *less* the executive.[23]

The problem of the system is most clearly seen in the centralization of power. More and more power is being centralized in a few large corporations and the federal government. Even the unions no longer represent their constituents. Radicals see centralization as leading to totalitarianism, the destruction of individual and community decisions. Oglesby restates this whole question as follows:

> The socialist radical, the corporatist conservative, and the welfare-state liberal are all equally capable of leading us forward into the totalized society. Whether central planning should be coordinated by government or corporate hands is a question whose realism has disappeared. The urgent question is about the locus of power in the community: Is it in the state or is it in the people?[24]

[23] *Ibid.*, pp. 7-8.
[24] Carl Oglesby and Richard Shaull, *Containment and Change* (New York: Macmillan, 1967), p. 164.

The New Left has very effectively used this analysis on the university and shown its subservience to the corporate enterprise. Why are universities such impersonal bureaucratic institutions? Because they rest on the same structures that support mass, dehumanized societies. They are first of all seen as supporting the establishment by providing research and newly trained personnel. They are governed by regents who are first of all businessmen, not educators. This was described most brilliantly by Clark Kerr, past president of the University of California.

> The university has become a prime instrument of national purpose. . . . This is the essence of the transformation now engulfing our universities. Basic to this transformation is the growth of the "knowledge industry," which is coming to permeate government and business. . . . What the railroads did for the second half of the 19th century and the automobile for the first half of this century, the knowledge industry may do for the second half of this century; that is, to serve as the focal point for national growth.[25]

The university is seen as an *industry*, as an instrument in the national purpose. But what if the students cannot agree with the national purpose? What has become of the spirit of free inquiry? Of the community of scholars? The government and corporatist control of the university is seen as another form of imperialism, a taking control of institutions that are weak and using them for purposes for which they were never intended. One can understand then how hypocritical it sounds when a university official tells demonstrators that the university should not take any position on the war, while that university presents lists of radicals to the F.B.I., receives defense contracts, and engages in biological and chemical warfare research.

This analysis is also extended to the Cold War, which is seen as a cover-up for many of the problems and evils of our society, a rationalization for protecting our power and richness, while yet maintaining a facade of righteousness. Thus in the name of anticommunism we can put down the rising expectations of the Third World and feel good about

---

[25] Quoted by Irving Howe, "Berkeley and Beyond," *New Republic*, CLII (May 1, 1965), p. 14.

it. The New Left has rejected anticommunism, for the term has lost its specific content and is used as a deterrent to building a new society here. It also is rejected because it subjugates all questioning and programs to the national interest.

This does not mean, however, that they are pro-communist. They see the Soviet Union as being a managed, undemocratic society, not unlike our own. The New Left people know the meaning of exploitation and totalitarianism. They understand the nature of fascist Germany or the repressive nature of Stalinism. They have read *1984* and *Brave New World*, but they see these same tendencies within our own society. And this they are protesting, not whitewashing. They simply don't see that much difference between Wall Street and the Kremlin. In the *Port Huron Statement* (p. 31) SDS declared:

> As democrats we are in basic opposition to the Communist system. The Soviet Union, as a system, rests on the total suppression of organized opposition, as well as a vision of the future in the name of which much human life has been sacrificed, and numerous small and large denials of human dignity rationalized. The Communist Party has equated falsely the "triumph of true socialism" with centralized bureaucracy. The Soviet state lacks independent labor organizations and other liberties we consider basic.

They are opposed to any totalitarianism, but they will not get involved in the Cold War. In fact, because of their democratic policy they refuse to exclude anyone from their groups. Jimmy Garrett illustrates this attitude in SNCC's newsletter, where he wrote:

> Man, the Communists, they're empty man, empty. They've got the same stale ideas, the same bureaucracy.... When he gets mixed up with us, a Commie dies and a person develops. They're not subverting us, we're subverting them.[26]

This managed society they describe is seen as resulting in alienation, a much more important concept than class struggle. They see the history of industrialization and urban-

[26] Quoted by Jack Newfield, "Revolt Without Dogma: The Student Left," *The Nation*, CC (May 10, 1965), p. 493.

ization as the story of man's increasing alienation from the decision-making process. Although man was freed from tradition, he did not find new freedom. As society became more highly centralized, he found himself subjected to society's structures and removed from control of them.[27] Tom Hayden describes this alienation as follows:

> Let's face it: all of us are corrupted or twisted by the conditions we face. Many people don't really believe they can get together. They've made endless accommodations to the system that is wasting them. A lot of people are trained to believe they're irrelevant.[28]

The *Port Huron Statement* also described this alienation (p. 7):

> Loneliness, estrangement, isolation describe the vast distance between man and man today. These dominant tendencies cannot be overcome by better personnel management, nor by improved gadgets, but only when a love of man overcomes the idolatrous worship of things by man.

This alienation affects all areas of life and destroys relationships and concern for one's fellow man. People are forced to turn to the tavern, the arts, or various means of escape to seek fulfillment. They cannot find it in the social order. This dilemma is illustrated by Jane Adams, a young SDS organizer, in her description of a factory.

> Each person is responsible to the "boss" above him, who is in turn responsible to the one above him, and so on up the bureaucracy. Human interaction between levels is almost nil, relationships are machine-like, but, because human beings are acting, and not machines, the interactions are fear-filled: One resents the "boss" above, because one does not like to be ordered around, does not like to have one's creativity and humanity denied; one fears the people one is boss of, because of understanding the resentment.[29]

Not only are people alienated, they are also excluded. The Negro, the poor white, the Spanish people, and the Indians

---

[27] Martin Oppenheimer, *Alienation or Participation: The Sociology of Participatory Democracy* ([Chicago]: Students for a Democratic Society, 1966), p. 1.

[28] Quoted by Ben Reade, "Prophet of the Powerless," *Renewal* (October-November, 1965), p. 20.

[29] Jane Adams, "People's Power," *New Left Notes*, January 20, 1967, p. 2.

have been shut out of the mainstream of American life. There are only three ways to get to the top: money, education, or knowing the right person. But for many people, none of these are possibilities. Automation only adds to this problem. Many who thought they were secure now find that they too have been disinherited.

In the eyes of the New Left, the system is so corrupt that it must be completely changed. They see little hope for reforming the system. It must be replaced. This is probably the fundamental difference between Liberalism and Radicalism. The liberal accepts the assumptions and needs of the establishment to be legitimate and thus chooses to work within the system to bring about the changes he sees as necessary. He accepts the assumption that the present system is able to change and solve our problems creatively. The liberal's norm for action is the system itself or at least what seems possible within the system. He thinks of all he could accomplish if he had control of the power structures. The radical rejects the very legitimacy of the establishment and doubts that meaningful change can be brought about through the existing structures. The radical maintains that the past thirty years have shown that the system cannot solve our problems. The radical knows that the system will not change unless it sees change to be in its own interest. An example of this difference in attitude may be given in relation to the poor. The liberal works for increased welfare benefits and other remedies, a program radicals see as increasing the powerlessness and dependency of the poor. The radical sees the need to change power relationships and the poor man's relationships to society.

This points to a difference in temperament between liberals and radicals. While the liberals talk about the credibility gap, the radicals speak of "damn lies." In regard to Vietnam, liberals tend to favor negotiations while radicals urge withdrawal. The New Left suspects that the liberals are first committed to respectability and only secondly to justice. The liberal is seen as one who wants to share in the affluence of the existing order, but is at the same time burdened with guilt feelings which he tries to assuage by disavowing its wrongs.

The New Left's analysis led radicals to break with the system, to separate themselves from it. They feel it is impossible to become a part of it without selling their souls. One radical told me that there is nothing wrong with a new house in the suburbs. The problem is what you have to do to get it, to earn that much money. Mario Savio, the Berkeley Free Speech leader, describes the feelings of the radical:

> And they find at one point or other that for them to become part of society, to become lawyers, ministers, businessmen, people in government, that very often they must compromise those principles which are most dear to them. They must suppress the most creative impulses that they have; this is a prior condition for becoming part of the system.[30]

They see those working within the system as having sold out to it. Their classic example is Hubert Humphrey. In the SDS *New Left Notes* there appeared a picture of Humphrey and General Ky with the following caption:

> The dilemma of American liberalism: former ADA leader Hubert Humphrey shown yuking it up with Nguyen Cao Ky, bloody dictator of the Saigon government at recent Honolulu conference. For men of deadened conscience, politics dces indeed make strange bedfellows.[31]

John Lewis, at the August 28, 1963 march on Washington for civil rights, told the crowd:

> My friends, let us not forget that we are engaged in a significant social revolution. By and large American politics is dominated by politicians who built their careers on immoral compromising and ally themselves with open forms of political, economic and social exploitation.[32]

The radicals believe our society is in deep trouble. They see our society being stagnated. Mario Savio described it as the bureaucratic belief that history has ended, that no further events can occur, that we must proceed as we are.[33] Already

---

[30] Mario Savio, "An End to History," in Jacobs and Landau, p. 233.
[31] *New Left Notes*, February 11, 1966, p. 1.
[32] Quoted by Murray Kempton, "The March on Washington," *New Republic*, CIL (September 14, 1963), p. 20.
[33] Jacobs and Landau, p. 231.

in the *Port Huron Statement*, SDS recognized the tragedy of our situation (p. 4):

> Not only did tarnish appear on our image of American virtue, not only did disillusion occur when the hypocrisy of American ideals was discovered, but we began to sense that what we had originally seen as the American Golden Age was actually the decline of an era.

Now with the threat of mass rebellion in our cities and the ever increasing predicament in Vietnam, radicals see little hope for the future of our system. They have set themselves on new paths. They have begun to prepare for a new society. They do not see the American establishment as being that powerful or effective. The world's most powerful army cannot conquer a small, developing nation; a large university feels compelled to call in state police to control a few dissident students rather than negotiate with them. A small demonstration causes a huge system to react with fear and repression. The establishment is seen as "running scared."

The New Left Value System

A common stereotype of the New Left is that they are too negative, protesting but never building, criticizing but never working to make things better. It is true that they are still an opposition movement and have not well defined their values. They are a group of people still in transition between two value systems, and are still reacting against authoritarianism, depersonalization, and exploitation. They are extremely critical, but they react against society because of their high ideals. What are those values which the New Left considers so important? Oglesby has stated that the purpose of the New Left is "to make love more possible."[34] They wish to remove from society those things which threaten and prevent love, justice, and community. They have a vision of a new society in which one can live creatively and find fulfillment.

The young radicals are activists and thus very suspicious

---

[34] Carl Oglesby, "Democracy is Nothing if it is Not Dangerous," undated reprint from *The Peacemaker*.

of any ideology. They are uninterested in the sectarian debates between Trotskyites and other left groups, for example. For them, action is more important than theory, issues more challenging than ideology. For a theoretical discussion to be relevant, it must be related to action. After a long philosophical dialogue with some New Left people, one explained that they were unaccustomed to such a theoretical discussion. He stated that my questions sounded something like a man walking into a carpenter shop and questioning the carpenter on why he uses wood. For them, faith is known by its works. They are interested in truth and action and are unconcerned about what labels may be attached to their insights.

Commitment is imperative for them. To be radical means first of all that one change his own life, that he live a radical life rather than be radical only when there is a demonstration. Paul Potter stated in his Washington speech that,

> By a social movement I mean more than petitions or letters of protest, or tacit support of dissident Congressmen; I mean people who are willing to change their lives, who are willing to challenge the system, to take the problem of change seriously.

They are interested in translating their moral values into politically relevant action. Ideals must be made concrete. Men are meant to live, not prepare to live. After listing some important ideals, Tom Hayden states that,

> These, however enthralling, are not worthy of our allegiance as abstractions. It is their infusion into practical life which gives them true content and determines the extent to which we shall value them.[35]

Their commitment means actively living those ideals they are working for.

There is a kind of moral purity in the witness of the New Left as illustrated in their emphasis on integrity, noncompromise, and the simple life. They stress integrity, honesty and authenticity over against phoniness and the hypocrisy of Brotherhood Week. In a dehumanized world, integrity of per-

---

[35] Tom Hayden, "A Letter to the New (Young) Left," *The New Student Left,* ed. Mitchell Cohen and Dennis Hale (Boston: Beacon Press, 1966), p. 6.

sons is seen as an essential. Thus they would rather be right than successful. They regularly use the phrase, "tell it like it is."

They maintain that morality and politics cannot be divided. The gross injustices of our day have taught them that ideals do have a place in political life. Thus they are most critical of liberals who would take a more pragmatic approach. They want politics to be what Jack Newfield has called "the art of the impossible."[36]

Compromise is a bad word in the New Left vocabulary. They have rejected the popular ethic of choosing the lesser of two evils. This became most clear to them after they had supported Johnson in 1964 because they considered him less evil than Goldwater. They see now that a vote for the lesser of two evils is truly the wasted vote. For them compromise is synonymous with "sell-out." They see this as no time to be compromising with the establishment. They must separate themselves from the establishment and create other alternatives, rather than operating on values and presuppositions they reject. This is partly due to their insight that the means cannot be separated from the ends, that evil means will bring about evil ends. The *Port Huron Statement* affirms this position (p. 6):

> If anything, the brutalities of the twentieth century teach us that means and ends are intimately related, that vague appeals to "posterity" cannot justify the mutilations of the present.

New Left people live what can be called the simple life. An example is the low living standards that movement workers have placed upon themselves. They see status, wealth, and success as meaningless goals. They reject the values of crass materialism, an attitude that transforms people into "consumers." They do not want to be forced into what Paul Goodman has described: "during my productive years I will spend eight hours a day doing what is no good."[37] The real issue is not the simple life, but priorities. What aids and what

---

[36] *Prophetic Minority*, p. 134.

[37] Paul Goodman, *Growing Up Absurd* (New York: Vintage Books, 1956), p. 29.

hinders in reaching the prize? Thus they have been freed from commonly expected status concerns and can work toward their vision of peace and justice.

This attitude also includes a healthy disdain for "respectability." They have felt free to grow beards and reject what middle-class America considers important. Steve Halliwell, an SDS staff worker, puts it more forcefully:

> Until the concern with respectability is overcome in an individual's own life, he will be unable to create a politics that deals with the fact of how unrespectable the fabric of American life is at present.[38]

This means caring more that others are being called "nigger" or that villages are being napalmed, than that we have the respect of society and are considered "nice guys."

At the center of New Left values is freedom. Negatively stated it is opposition to authoritarianism, paternalism, manipulation and institutionalism. In this they are the products of the enlightenment, children of Voltaire, Rousseau, and Jefferson. But they were also influenced by the conservative tradition of Herbert Spencer and William G. Sumner. They reject the paternalism of the *in loco parentis* policy of the universities, the compulsion of the draft and the oppression of American class structures.

Freedom for the radical means that people have the right to participate in making the decisions that affect their lives. This is very different from the conservative view of liberty as the right to do what one wants. The radical does not see freedom as including the liberty to violate other human beings. The conservative sees a tension between equality and freedom, but the radical sees one to be impossible without the other. They go hand in hand. As seen by the New Left, America has never had either. We have had laissez-faire capitalism and the "freedom" to exploit other people, but never freedom and equality. Freedom must mean more than "freedom" for economic self-interest.

This means developing a sense of independence in people

---

[38] Steve Halliwell, "Personal Liberation and Social Change," *New Politics News/2* [August, 1967], p. 13.

rather than a feeling of dependence on the state. This was emphasized in the *Port Huron Statement* (pp. 6-7):

> The goal of man and society should be human independence: a concern not with image or popularity but with finding a meaning in life that is personally authentic; a quality of mind not compulsively driven by a sense of powerlessness, nor one which unthinkingly adopts status values, nor one which represses all threats to its habits, but one which has full, spontaneous access to present and past experiences, one which easily unites the fragmented parts of personal history, one which openly faces problems which are troubling and unresolved; one with an intuitive awareness of possibilities, an active sense of curiosity, an ability and willingness to learn. This kind of independence does not mean egotistical individualism — the object is not to have one's way so much as it is to have a way that is one's own.

This means more than a negative freedom. It means also the freedom to develop one's potential. It is the freedom to live responsibly. It is an openness to new possibilities. It means more than choosing between alternatives established by someone else.

They would apply their antiauthoritarian ethic to every aspect of society, to all groups. In an article on leadership, an SDS chapter president discusses the role of leadership in an authoritarian society. He concludes that a group should have no permanent officers, or at the most rotating chairmen for meetings and a coordinator for each activity. He argues that leadership is based on authoritarian premises and blocks each person in the group from decision making and personal responsibility.[39]

We must now look at what the New Left would put in the place of our authoritarian structures. First, however, it must be said that they reject the idea of setting up any blueprints for what society should be like in the future. This would only be imposing another authoritarian structure. Whatever develops must come from the people, not from a group of radical intellectuals. They do have some idea of where they are going, however. Since they are disturbed by the increasing centralization of power and decision making, they are

---

[39] Henry W. Haslach, "Thoughts on Leadership," *New Left Notes,* June 26, 1967, p. 4.

agreed that society must be decentralized. They would increase the number of centers of decision making and restore the ability of people to have a voice in the decision-making processes. Their term for this is participatory democracy. This means that everyone should be able to participate in making the decisions that affect his life. The *Port Huron Statement* set forth this approach (p. 7):

> As a *social system* we seek the establishment of a democracy of individual participation, governed by two central aims: that the individual share in those social decisions determining the quality and direction of his life; that society be organized to encourage independence in men and provide the media for their common participation.

They see institutions as being legitimate only when those institutions come out of the voluntary participation of the people who will be affected by them. That means that in relation to an urban renewal project, those who will be affected by it will help determine its nature and even if it will be instituted at all. In relation to student power, it means that students will participate in making any decisions that affect them, rather than being arbitrarily ruled by the administration. In a factory it would mean that the workers would help control the factory. Decisions must be made in the context of free association. Therefore, the best kind of government is not one to which people give their hopes and fears and expect it to be the custodian of conscience and the national good, a benevolent chief magistrate. Rather, government should come from the people. They themselves should freely make the social contract.

The New Left believes that people are able to govern themselves. This opposition to centralization is very similar to conservative political philosophy, but for very different reasons. Conservatism takes this stand on the basis of individualism, each man for himself. Participatory democracy, on the other hand, is founded upon a profound understanding of community. Politics is seen as serving the function of building community and bringing people out of isolation. Their understanding of community is based on their experience of community in the movement. It is derived from their together being beaten by police, sharing jail cells, and their struggle to find consensus within their groups. Since they experienced community, they believe the good society is possible. Jane Stembridge, who helped organize SNCC, describes this view of community:

> ... finally it all boils down to human relationships. It has nothing to do finally with governments. It is the question of whether we ... whether *I* shall go on living in isolation or whether there shall be a *we*. The student movement is not a cause ... it is a collision between this one person and that one person. It is a *I am going to sit beside you*. ... Love alone is radical. Political statements are not; programs are not; even going to jail is not. ... [40]

The New Left is a deep expression of humanitarianism. They would replace competition with cooperation and profit with the service motif. They realize that it is not necessary for society to be based on dog-eat-dog competition. They know that there are other possibilities. They would place human rights above property rights. They would see personal relationships as more important than functional relationships. They seek justice for all men and dream of a nonviolent society, where violence and brutality will not be the order of the day. Although most are not now pacifists, they have rejected violence ultimately as a way of life. The *Port Huron Statement* affirmed these goals (p. 7): "We would replace power rooted in possession, privileged [sic], or circumstance by power and uniqueness rooted in love, reflectiveness, reason and creativity." They believe that society can be a shared humanity and concern for each other, and not just protecting a person from his neighbor.

For the New Left, man is central. He must be an end and not a means. Thus they reject the Russian and American notion that the individual exists for the state. He is not something to be manipulated. In Buber's term, man is to be treated as a Thou rather than an it. Participatory democracy assumes a high doctrine of man, that he has great potential for good.

---

[40] Quoted by Howard Zinn, *SNCC: The New Abolitionists* (Boston: Beacon Press, 1964), p. 7.

It assumes that people are capable of understanding their problems and able to participate in their solution. They reject the contention that only a privileged few can be independent. Apathy is not an inherent part of man, but rather is rooted in the depersonalizing nature of our social institutions. An authoritarian structure does not develop independent people. Therefore, they believe that people can become involved in the decision-making process and overcome their alienation. The *Port Huron Statement* affirmed this hope in man (p. 6):

> We oppose, too, the doctrine of human incompetence because it rests essentially on the modern fact that men have been "competently" manipulated into incompetence — we see little reason why men cannot meet with increasing skill the complexities and responsibilities of their situation, if society is organized not for minority, but for majority, participation in decision-making.

They recognize man's capacity for evil. They have seen too much of the evils of our society to have a Pollyanna view of the world. They understand brutality and exploitation. However, they wish to appeal to man's potential for creativity, freedom, and love. There is an awareness that we now have the technical ability to overcome poverty if we would only use it. Thus they are pessimistic about our present, but optimistic about the possibilities for the future.

Their concern for man is also shown in that they see salvation not only in terms of social structures, but also in relation to man himself. They see the need to begin by changing their own lives. Since they believe that important needs are personal, they hope to develop a sense of worth and dignity in each person, for otherwise a person cannot act independently of the system. As one SNCC worker wrote, the goal is "... to build a society where the problems of the individual can never be forgotten, a world where understanding and love are the keys to success."[41] It is implied in Oglesby's statement that "only men, not states, can be free, can produce and exhibit freedom."[42]

---

[41] Quoted by Bruce Payne, "SNCC: An Overview Two Years Later," in Cohen and Hale, p. 84.

[42] *Containment and Change*, p. 163.

A short word should be said regarding history. The student revolt means a radical break from a mood of inevitability. Although they see no particular direction in history, they do have a tremendous hope for the future. Progress also is not inevitable, but they keep working with the hope that the revolution will come, that a new era will dawn. They know that they cannot decide the future. Thus they have no fixed notion of what the future holds, no dogmatic plans that they will try to enforce. When the revolution comes, then the people must decide. The future remains open.

Strategy for Social Change

How is it that the radical hopes to bring change and what is the nature of that change? As was noted above, they are not interested in setting up new structures to impose on society. Unlike the doctrinaire Marxist-Leninists and the Old Left, they do not presume to know what is good for the people. They do know, however, that meaningful change must mean a change of the whole system. They are talking about revolution, not reform, for they see the history of reform in America as the story of the defeat of radical goals. They are not interested in patchwork on the present system. Thus SNCC has rejected the goals of integration. They are not as interested in working toward better jobs and housing as they are in helping people to build community, to be free, and to build new values. They see little validity in helping black people become a part of a sick white society. They would rather build a new society. As Carmichael explains it,

> . . . Integration speaks not at all to the problem of poverty, only to the problem of blackness. Integration today means the man who "makes it," leaving his black brothers behind in the ghetto as fast as his new sports car will take him.[43]

They seek a new society organized on completely new lines.

How shall they work toward that goal? How will the revolution come? How shall they relate to the present establishment? The prior question is whether you think the system is bad, or whether you think meaningful change can come

---

[43] Stokely Carmichael, "What We Want," in Cohen and Hale, p. 113.

by putting different people into office. If you believe the latter, you simply try to find better men. This is the liberal approach, a search for reform and the lesser evil. But if you believe the former, then your primary goal is not to support the system, but to undermine it. The radical separates himself from the system he wishes to confront (for example, segregation) so that he no longer gives any support to that structure. They do not want to participate in what they are trying to oppose. Steve Halliwell notes that,

> In the personal lives of SDS members, the break with ties to authoritarian institutions and the creation of a radical stance is closely tied to a rejection of conventional politics of pressure and persuasion for amelioration of social injustices; in other words, people who recognize the political process as perverted will not seek change through the institutions that process has created.[44]

The goal of the New Left is not to become the establishment, but to eliminate it. Their vision of society does not include an establishment.

Basically they feel it is naive to think that one can bring meaningful change from within. If you are in the system, you need to adopt its values, play by its rules. If not, you are either crushed or pushed aside. Those who decide to work within by use of compromise to reach their goals are seen as having sold out. Radicals also consider this approach to be based on undemocratic presuppositions. It assumes that one effects change by getting oneself into the structure. It does not recognize that change needs to come from the people — not just better people in the system, but constituencies that will demand change in the system.

Change, they say, does not originate in establishment channels. A social revolution cannot be carried out in the courtroom, although this may help. From their perspective, the Emancipation Proclamation was not what freed the slaves; it was the result of Abolitionist agitation. The 1946 Supreme Court decision declaring segregation in interstate transportation unconstitutional did not integrate the bus terminals; it took the Freedom Rides to do that. The 1954 school deseg-

---

[44] Halliwell, p. 12.

regation decision of the Supreme Court has not integrated the schools. Change must come out of the community. They are aware of how a few Black students could walk into a Southern drug store for a cup of coffee and shake the very foundation of Southern civilization by that act. This helps shape their theory of social change.

Some radicals do not completely reject working within the structure if one is clear what his purposes are. One can work within as a guerilla in order to undermine the system, but not to bring change through it. One can enter electoral politics, but only as a tool by which to educate the public as to the nature of the system we live under. This approach does not include operating on the basis of establishment values or compromise in order to reach one's ends. Carl Davidson illustrates this approach in writing about the university.

> Fighting for reforms and making a revolution should not be seen as mutually exclusive positions. The question should be: what kind of reforms move us toward a radical transformation of both the university and society in general? First of all, we should avoid the kinds of reforms which leave the basic *rationale* of the system unchallenged. For instance, a bad reform to work for would be getting a better grading system, because the underlying rationale — the need for grades at all — remains unchallenged.[45]

The New Left is convinced that social change should start from the bottom. Their alternative to centralized power is to build up democratic organizations in the community which will begin to take power and allow people again to participate in decision making. They are opposed to the elitist approach which sees change coming from the top down. This they consider undemocratic and feeding into the establishment mentality. Although the New Left hopes to build a new society, radicals reject the idea of setting up any blueprints for what society should be like in the future. This would only be imposing another authoritarian structure. Thus they have no fixed notion of what the future holds, no dogmatic plans that they will try to enforce. The future remains open. Their

---

[45] Carl Davidson, *The Multiversity: Crucible of the New Working Class* (Chicago: Students for a Democratic Society, 1967), p. 13.

slogan is "let the people decide." Tom Hayden develops this idea:

> The emphasis in the movement on "letting the people decide," on decentralized decision-making, on refusing alliances with top leaders, stems from the need to create a personal and group identity that can survive both the temptations and the crippling effects of this society. Power in America is abdicated by individuals to top-down organizational units, and it is in the recovery of this power that the movement becomes distinct from the rest of the country and a new kind of man emerges.[46]

Therefore they are organizing community organizations among the poor, working for local democracy in unions, and organizing against the war at local and university levels. Their purpose is not to become powerful but to distribute power by people taking power over their own lives. They see grassroots organizing as the answer.

This raises the question of the agent of social change. Through what group of people do they see these changes taking place? For the Old Left the working class was the focus of organizing and hope. But now that industrial unionism has succeeded, it is clear to the New Left that what has happened is the creation of a new conservative, self-centered, privileged class. They have a deep distrust of organized labor because of, among many other things, its exclusion of Negroes, support of the Cold War, and undemocratic tactics. The New Left turns mainly to the university and to the poor. They turn to the university partly because that is their home, and because it is the place where a large percentage of Americans rework their values. Recently, they have also begun to organize among what they call the "new working class," the professionals and white-collar workers.

For the most part, however, they have turned to the poor, for they assume that those most deprived are those most ready to change society. Todd Gitlin, an organizer among the white poor, writes:

> ...People strongly afflicted with the rottenness of our society are best capable of exorcising that rot. The process of social change must involve the movement of masses of people. Movement be-

---

comes meaningful when the people directly afflicted organize for change, for it is then that people are sensing their own possibilities as men, their power to make things happen. The poor know they are poor and don't like it; hence they can be organized to demand an end to poverty and the construction of a decent social order.[47]

Their hope is to bring power back into the poor communities and thereby begin to establish the new forms they dream of. They are implementing this through the building of community organizations, tenant unions, and welfare recipients unions. They are seeking to build new radical constituencies rather than work through coalition with other groups, partly because they do not know with whom to join. They cannot look to labor, liberal groups, or either major political party. They see that they must go their own way.

Their approach is a long-range strategy. Since they see a long struggle in the future, they can plan their actions accordingly. This means that there is no one single issue that must be won. Rather than taking a single-issue approach to social change, they seek a wholistic approach, trying to see any one issue within the context of the total structures. In organizing, they look for specific instances that will point out to the public how little control they have over the basic decisions that affect their lives. Personal problems are shown to be linked with social issues. They try to show people what the capitalist system is doing to their lives. They illustrate how elected officials are basically not interested in what their constituency thinks. They seek to expose the basic political principles upon which the system operates and try to help people to become free from the institutions that control them. Thus they try to desanctify and delegitimatize the sacred cows of our society, for once a person no longer respects those institutions, they no longer have power over his life. This means seeking to make alienation more obvious and to transform that alienation into disaffection in order to waken people from their apathy. The goal is liberation from all that enslaves people.

---

[47] Todd Gitlin, "The Battlefields and the War," in Cohen and Hale, p. 126.

The New Left arose out of the Civil Rights Movement and the Peace Movement. They were baptized into the philosophy of nonviolence through suffering at the hands of the police. Basically, they are nonviolent and against militarism. In its founding statement, SDS stated:

> In social change or interchange, we find violence to be abhorrent because it requires generally the transformation of the target, be it a human being or a community of people, into a depersonalized object of hate. It is imperative that the means of violence be abolished and the institutions — local, national, international — that encourage non-violence as a condition of conflict be developed.[48]

However, even though a large part of the early New Left was pacifist, pacifists today are a minority in the movement. For another minority there is a tendency to romanticize violence. With mounting frustrations and repressions, many are not willing to exclude the use of violence in social change. Their sympathies are with the rebellions in the Black communities. Already in 1961, Tom Hayden wrote that nonviolence will be dissipated if it is not soon secured in new social structures.[49] Che Guevara is becoming more of a hero than Gandhi. The future remains unclear on this issue. Pacifists like Staughton Lynd are still active and respected in the movement, however. Possibly the main reason for the rejection of pacifism is that most pacifist spokesmen are liberals. The New Left stands in crisis on this point. It may mean a basic compromise of the New Left vision, and even its demise, should violence become the main tool for social change, as advocated by a few.

The most profound aspect of the New Left strategy of social change is their decision to point to the new while the old is being destroyed. They realize that finally to be radical means that one lives a radical life. Bruce Payne expresses this view.

> Community organizers need to take even more seriously the new left dictum that one should try to live now as if the good society

---

[48] *Port Huron Statement,* p. 8.
[49] Cohen and Hale, p. 7.

were already here — to show by example the style and quality of life for which we are working.[50]

This means that one should live as if the revolution were already here, that the present power structures have no power over one's life. Their purpose is to create new alternatives, to show society what the possibilities are. This means the creation of parallel structures to counter the old structures, to set up a viable, moral counterpart. These are seen as a method of challenging the system, of showing the system for what it is. It is a demonstration of alternatives and a way to attract new people into the movement. Examples of these new structures are the free universities that are found on the fringe of many universities. It means underground newspapers to counter the establishment press. It means independent political parties like the Mississippi Freedom Democratic Party. It is the creation of children's communities to replace our present school system. It is the setting up of communal living to overcome the alienation and depersonalization of our mass society. Already the New Left is concretely setting their ideal into action.

Evaluation

The New Left has made an excellent analysis of society. The young radicals have correctly understood the corporate nature of the system and how it operates. Their analysis has not been successfully refuted. Their alternative of decentralization and participatory democracy seems imperative in our increasingly totalitarian society. They have a profound understanding of how sin (alienation) is a product of our social structures. They fail to recognize, however, that sin also has personal roots. Sin is due to more than social structures, for it is man who built those repressive structures. Their vision of salvation, however, has both the personal and social aspects. They see the need for the individual to change his own life, first of all to become radical himself. The problems of sin, conflict, and alienation have not yet been overcome, as can be evidenced by the struggles involved in any New

---

[50] *Ibid.*, p. 95.

Left meeting. It seems important, then, that they should have a deeper understanding of the personal roots of alienation.

Part of the power of the New Left is in its eschatological vision, the dream of man and the world as they could be. The radicals cannot be criticized at this point. However, they are weak in that they do not have an adequate basis for their values, vision, and goals. To rely mainly on experience has proven in the past to end in rationalization. Experience is not that trustworthy. They have no adequate basis for self-criticism. The young radical needs a firmer basis for his non-compromising obedience.

Partly because of this lack of a solid basis, many activists often become discouraged and drop out, or their attitudes harden with bitterness. There seem to be two dangers that they face. Either they can be so dedicated to principle that they become irrelevant, or they can be so contextual and rooted in what is that they no longer have anything to contribute. They must avoid both of these tendencies. One is based in the desire to remain pure, the other in the temptation to compromise on the means for a short-term goal.

One cannot criticize them for being naive idealists, for they have truly seen man at his worst. They know what man is, they have experienced that, but yet they have a vision of what man could be. They take eschatology seriously. It is interesting to note that the "realist" arguments against the New Left are the same arguments that are used against pacifists and other reformers. It has not been proven that the idealists are less in touch with reality than the realists. The problem of the New Left is not idealism, but the very opposite. Whenever one decides to follow his ideals seriously, the danger is moralism, pride, and self-righteousness. One begins to set oneself over against the other. A Manichean division between black and white, good and evil, appears. This results in an intolerance of opposing opinions and even in paranoia, a distrust and suspicion of all outsiders as the enemy. While for the most part the New Left has maintained a real openness, these tendencies do exist.

What will become of the New Left? Will it result in a new era or is it doomed to oblivion along with many other movements? Will it become completely dominated by Old Left dogmatism, or can it maintain the vision described above? Can it avoid both Stalinism and the temptation to sell out? We do know that this small minority of activists has had a significant impact on our nation. The administration cannot run the Vietnam war without contending with them and even publicly answering them. They have successfully raised important issues. Perhaps if the radicals will take two steps forward, the rest of society will take one. A good example of pulling others to the left is the way SNCC has forced the NAACP out of the courtroom and into the streets. What will happen to the New Left if it continues to grow? Can it still remain a *creative* minority? What is at stake is not some radical organization such as SDS, but the vision of a liberated community. It is too early to decide whether it will have a lasting impact or be a passing mood. One hopes it will be more than a small flicker of light in the darkness.

CHAPTER TWO

Anabaptism:
A Sixteenth-Century Analogy

We must obey God rather than men.
The Apostle Peter

Introduction

Out of personal involvement in the New Left has come a
new appreciation for the radical heritage of the Christian
faith in general and the Anabaptist tradition in particular.
Although raised in the Church of the Brethren,[1] I was un-
aware of the radical nature of this tradition until I had had
contact with the New Left. The beard of the protester gave
me a new appreciation for my Anabaptist grandfather's beard.
His beard symbolizes for him something very similar to what
the beard means for the protester. When I asked my grandfather why he grew a beard his reply was that it was to
show that he was different from the world. The beard of the
protester is to demonstrate that he is not a part of the establishment. My own beard is a conscious attempt to bring
together these two radical perspectives.

The stimulus for the comparison of these two movements

---

[1] One of the three historic peace churches, along with the Quakers
and the Mennonites.

came from Staughton Lynd, who in describing the New Left wrote:

> What is most clear at the moment is the call reminiscent of the Radical Reformation to "come out of Babylon." Let the teacher leave the university and teach in Freedom Schools; let the reporter quit his job on a metropolitan daily and start a community newspaper; generally, let the intellectual make insurgency a full-time rather than a part-time occupation.[2]

The basic premise of this chapter is that there is a close similarity between the New Left and the "Radical Reformation"[3] of the sixteenth century, or what is sometimes referred to as the "Left Wing of the Reformation."[4] This comparison will be made by using an outline for Chapter Two similar to that of Chapter One, thereby showing the parallels between these two movements.

The Radical Reformation is a diverse opposition to the Reformation led by Luther, Zwingli, and Calvin, and can be divided into four distinct groups: the Anabaptists, Revolutionaries, Spiritualizers, and the Anti-Trinitarians (Evangelical Rationalists).[5] The focus of this study will be upon the Anabaptists and will deal only in passing with the other groups, even though there would be similarities with them also. The term "Anabaptists" includes the Swiss Brethren, South German Anabaptists, Dutch Mennonites, and the Hutterites. Thus the term does not include Thomas Müntzer and other revolutionaries, for from the beginning the Anabaptists condemned the revolutionaries for their use of violence.[6] As will be seen, Müntzer hardly fits the description of Anabaptism found in this chapter. It must be stated, however, that in a few cases such as in Münster (1534-1535),

---

[2] Staughton Lynd, *The New Radicals and Participatory Democracy*, reprinted from *Dissent* (Summer, 1965) by Students for a Democratic Society, Chicago, p. 5.

[3] The term used by George Williams, *The Radical Reformation* (Philadelphia: Westminster Press, 1962).

[4] The term popularized by Roland Bainton, "The Left Wing of the Reformation," *Journal of Religion*, XXI (April, 1941), pp. 124-134.

[5] Franklin H. Littell, *The Origins of Sectarian Protestantism* (New York: Macmillan, 1964), pp. 43-45.

[6] *Ibid.*, p. 11.

Anabaptists overtaken with apocalypticism did lead violent revolutions and tried to establish the "New Jerusalem" through force. Radicalism does have within itself the seeds of this action, for if one expects God to usher in the kingdom, it is easy for one to become disillusioned and try to bring it in oneself. Although the enemies of Anabaptism used the Münster fiasco to discredit all of the movement, a more correct evaluation is given by John Howard Yoder, a Mennonite theologian.

> ... The revolution of Münster, with which uninformed historians still blacken the Anabaptist name, was not consistent Anabaptism; it was a reversion to the same heresy accepted by Lutherans and Catholics alike — the belief that political means can be used against God's enemies to oblige an entire society to do God's will.[7]

From the beginning the Anabaptists were misunderstood and portrayed unfairly. Even the term "Anabaptist" is a derogatory name meaning "re-baptizer." They themselves rejected this term, since although they practiced adult baptism, they never considered infant baptism to be any baptism at all. Following Luther and Zwingli, scholars have described this movement with scorn and an obvious lack of objectivity. Engels and Kautsky took the movement seriously and saw in it a manifestation of the class struggle and the forerunner of Marxism, but failed to see its religious basis.[8] However, in this century, especially due to the work of Mennonite historians, a new surge of interest and appreciation has emerged with the result that Anabaptism is now being taken seriously as a legitimate alternative to the conservative Reformation led by Luther, Zwingli, and Calvin. It is now seen as a group that dared to challenge the assumptions of over a thousand years of European history and its cultural synthesis called *Corpus Christianum*, a medieval combination of religious, political, and economic interests.

---

[7] John Howard Yoder, *Peace Without Eschatology?* (Scottdale, Pa.: Mennonite Publishing House, 1954), p. 15.

[8] Gerhard Zschäbitz, an East German scholar, has made a much more objective analysis of Anabaptism and has modified the views of Engels. *Zur Mitteldeutschen Wiedertäuferbewegung nach dem Grossen Bauernkrieg* (Berlin: Rütten und Loeing, 1958).

Historical Background

As one reads sixteenth-century history, one is impressed with the parallels to our own century. There were the liberals who decided to work through the system and thus moderated their views so as not to offend the town council (Zwingli). There were the fiery revolutionaries (Müntzer) who preached violent overthrow of the system and the establishment of a just order composed of the disinherited. There were the conservatives (Luther) who defended the status quo and advocated brutal suppression of the peasants who refused to submit to further oppression. It was a time of revolutionary ferment, but the revolution was aborted. The peasant uprisings were effectively crushed. The Catholic Church suffered from a centralization of power in its bureaucracy. The Holy Roman Empire had already begun to crumble. It was an era of decline. William Estep, a Baptist scholar, in his description of the Anabaptists notes:

> The sixteenth century was dark because it was the product of previous centuries. Civilization had become increasingly oblivious to human suffering and the value of the individual. Piety was evaluated by the amount of accumulated external acts. Hypocrisy became the hallmark of the age. In the darkness the Anabaptists shone like so many meteors against the night.[9]

It was more than a period of decline, however. It was also a time of hope sparked by the new humanism of the Renaissance. Reformation was seen as a true possibility. But for many, these hopes were short-lived. Although Zwingli had at first opposed infant baptism, he soon realized that this view was not compatible with the maintenance of a church establishment. At the end of the second Zürich disputation, October 1523, Zwingli maintained that no reforms should be instituted without the approval of the magistracy.[10] This was cause for much disappointment among Zwingli's more radical followers and led to a split with his reformation.

By the end of 1524, groups were meeting in homes in

---

[9] William R. Estep, *The Anabaptist Story* (Nashville, Tenn.: Broadman Press, 1963), p. 20.

[10] Williams, p. 90.

Zürich for Bible study and discussion. Soon they had decided not to have their infants baptized. On the evening of January 21, 1525, three days after the town council had declared that all who refused to have their infants baptized would be exiled, the first adult baptism was performed. After prayer and discussion, George Blaurock, a former priest, declared he wanted to be baptized. After he was baptized, he baptized the others in the room. This was the beginning of the first Anabaptist congregation.[11] This dedicated group began preaching everywhere they went, proclaiming their new vision. The movement spread rapidly to South Germany, North Germany, and the Netherlands, and into Austria and Moravia, for the time was ripe for their message.

Although there was an enthusiastic response to their preaching, they were soon met with persecution. Zwingli realized the threat the Anabaptists posed to his reformation, and urged stern measures against them. On November 19, 1526, the Zürich Council passed a law making it punishable by death not only to rebaptize, but also even to attend Anabaptist preaching.[12] Soon afterward, Felix Mantz was drowned in the river at Zürich while his family and friends stood by the river and urged him to remain steadfast. He became the first "Protestant" martyr to die at the hands of the Protestants.[13] Persecution soon became intense. In Swabia (South Germany), four hundred police were hired to find the Anabaptists and were ordered to execute them without trial. This group proved to be too small and was strengthened to one thousand.[14] One famous executioner of the time, Berthold Aichele of Bavaria, proudly boasted that he had hanged twelve hundred revolutionaries and over forty pastors.[15] The following account has been preserved of the martyrdom of Michael Sattler. After a trial where he fearlessly defended his faith, he received his sentence.

---

[11] *Ibid.*, p. 120.
[12] *Ibid.*, p. 144.
[13] *Ibid.*, p. 146.
[14] Estep, p. 46.
[15] Littell, p. 71.

> ... Judgment is passed that Michael Sattler shall be delivered to the executioner, who shall lead him to the place of execution and cut out his tongue, then forge him fast to a wagon and thereon with red-hot tongs twice tear pieces from his body; and after he has been brought outside the gate, he shall be plied five times more in the same manner.... [16]

The account of this event relates that

> After this had been done in the manner prescribed, he was burned to ashes as a heretic. His fellow brethren were executed with the sword, and the sisters drowned. His wife, also after being subjected to many entreaties, admonitions, and threats, under which she remained steadfast, was drowned a few days afterward. Done the 21st day of May, A.D. 1527.[17]

This persecution failed to stop the movement, however. The Anabaptists were willing to die for their faith, and prayed only that they would remain faithful. The Count of Altzey was reported to have said: "What shall I do, the more I execute, the more they increase."[18]

Motivating Factors Behind the Anabaptists

The movement began with intellectuals who were trained in the humanist tradition of Erasmus, and who had worked closely with Zwingli's reformation attempt. Probably most important was the humanist emphasis on biblical studies. The most obvious factor was that they began to take the Christian tradition seriously and soon saw that the Catholic Church and the Reformation were not meeting the standards of biblical faith. They were not anti-Christian, but they thought the established church was. They were convinced that the Christian message was relevant, and that it should be lived rather than compromised for political expediency. They believed what their Bible study had forced them to conclude, and thus began to put their faith into action.

They were people who had tried to bring reforms, but their suggestions were rejected. They sought public discus-

---

[16] Quoted by George Williams, *Spiritual and Anabaptist Writers*, Vol. XXV: *Library of Christian Classics* (Philadelphia: Westminster Press, 1957), p. 143.

[17] *Ibid.*, pp. 143-144.

[18] Estep, p. 46.

sions (disputations) whenever possible; but their reforms would have meant disestablishment, as will be noted below. They soon learned that meaningful change was not possible within the system. Soon they, like the New Left, were forced to take the sectarian route of working outside the establishment.

There has been much debate regarding what was the central concern of the Anabaptists. Littell sees it as the attempt to reinstitute the "True Church," patterned after the life style of the early church. The restitution of New Testament Christianity then would be the center of the movement.[19] Harold S. Bender, the Mennonite historian, sees the central thrust as discipleship and obedience to Christ, which results in a church that is a brotherhood and in an ethic of love and nonresistance.[20] Bender is more accurate, for it seems that the attempt to recover primitive Christianity is actually a result of discipleship. While orthodoxy implied that the Bible is ambiguous, the Anabaptists taught that it is clear in regard to both the content of Christian faith and the demands on a Christian community. They believed the biblical vision to be worth living, and they proceeded to live it.

The Anabaptist Analysis of Society

As has been noted above, the Anabaptists were disturbed by the condition of the church. They accepted the view that the church had "fallen" and was no longer the true church described in the New Testament. The basis for Littell's argument, that restitution was at the center of Anabaptist thought, is that they saw the church as fallen. They adapted the fall of man to the history of the church. Most Anabaptists dated the fall of the church with the reign of Constantine (313-337), although some would put the date earlier.[21] The important issue here is the union of church and state and the end of the church as a voluntary association of believers. It was

---

[19] Littell, pp. XVI-XVII.

[20] Harold S. Bender, "The Anabaptist Vision," *Recovery of the Anabaptist Vision*, ed. Guy S. Hershberger (Scottdale, Pa.: Herald Press, 1957), p. 42.

[21] Littell, p. 63.

the transformation of Christianity from a personal faith and a movement into an obligatory state religion.[22] They were protesting the transformation of religion into an establishment serving the ends of the state.

The Anabaptists had a clear doctrine of the state. There was little doubt among most of them that the state *(Obrigkeit)* is ordained by God. The task of the state was considered to be closely connected with its origin. It had existed from the beginning of creation with God as the ruler. After the fall of man, however, this office was given to man. The state, then, must be understood in light of man's sin. God gave man the state because of his sin. Riedemann, an early Hutterite, puts this quite strongly.

> It is therefore obvious that the state is not given out of grace, but out of punishment and wrath. And this is due to the alienation of the people when they forsook God and followed the flesh. Therefore they must be ruled by the flesh.[23]

Most Anabaptists, however, did not feel quite this negative about the authorities. Most would say the state was given as an act of grace, for the giving of the state was seen as God's desire not to allow man to go to the last consequence of his sin. As one Anabaptist put it, "Where there was no state, it would be impossible to live."[24] Thus government is for man's protection, for the preservation of order. Its purpose was seen to be to protect the innocent and weak from evildoers, to maintain peace and order. In the Zofingen disputation of 1532, the spokesman for the Swiss Brethren stated:

> We grant that in the non-Christian world state authorities have a legitimate place, to keep order, to punish the evil, and to protect the good. But we as Christians live according to the Gospel and our only authority and Lord is Jesus Christ.[25]

They made no theological distinction between a just and

---

[22] *Ibid.*, p. 64.

[23] Quoted by Hans J. Hillerbrand, *Die politische Ethik des oberdeutschen Täufertums* (Leiden: E. J. Brill, 1960), p. 11 (my translation).

[24] *Ibid.*, p. 9.

[25] Quoted by Harold S. Bender, "The Pacifism of the Sixteenth Century Anabaptists," *Church History*, XXIV (1955), p. 122.

unjust government, for their relation to the state was independent from the moral nature of the government.[26] The government itself was not the judge of their relation to it. They maintained that a godless government is just as ordained of God as is a "good" government, but that a good government also stands outside the "fullness of Christ."[27]

However, for the Anabaptists, the authority of the state was limited. They were agreed that the state had no authority in matters of faith. It could have nothing to do with the inner man. At this point there was a sharp disagreement between them and the mainline reformers. During Sattler's trial he referred to the judges as the servants of God. Thus he recognized their authority, but at the same time maintained that they had no authority over religious matters.[28] We see here a very firm basis for their position of separation of church and state, a very radical position for that day, and a view they never gave up. As late as 1589, they declared in the Zürich City Council: "The state authorities have no place in the Church of God, no right to control and persecute the conscience."[29] We see then that the state was recognized as having authority in an evil world, but that the authority for the Anabaptists was not the state, but Christ. As will be noted below, the Anabaptists felt no responsibility for the state.

The Anabaptist doctrine of the state rests on a two-kingdom dualism which makes a sharp distinction between the kingdom of Christ and the kingdom of this world. To understand it better, let us first look at Luther's two kingdoms. This view acknowledges both Christ's rule and the kingdom of this world, but maintains that the two cannot be distinguished. Luther's two kingdoms are really one. They are "two different

[26] Hans J. Hillerbrand, "The Anabaptist View of the State," *Mennonite Quarterly Review*, XXXII (April, 1958), pp. 92-93.

[27] Hillerbrand, *Die politische Ethik des oberdeutschen Täufertums*, pp. 12-13.

[28] Gustav Bossert, Jr., "Michael Sattler's Trial and Martyrdom in 1527," *Mennonite Quarterly Review*, XXV (July, 1951), p. 209.

[29] Harold S. Bender, "The Anabaptists and Religious Liberty in the 16th Century," *Mennonite Quarterly Review*, XXIX (April, 1955), p. 91.

modes of divine rule." Of those who accept Christ's rule,
Luther states:

> These need neither worldly sword nor law. And if all the world
> were made up of true Christians, there would be no need for
> ruler, king, lord, sword or law — for the Holy Spirit which they
> have in their hearts teaches them and brings it about that they
> wrong no one, but love all and suffer evil voluntarily and cheer-
> fully from anyone. Therefore it is impossible that worldly sword
> and law would have anything to do among Christians.[30]

With this statement, any Anabaptist could agree. The big difference between the two comes when Luther states that God
rules over both kingdoms with different standards. The Christian for Luther has dual citizenship and thus must live by
two sets of standards.[31] The Christian must live in both realms.

The Anabaptists, however, separate the two realms. For
them, Christ brought in a new kingdom and a new life for
those who follow him. Those who wish to follow him cannot
be in both kingdoms at the same time. This is an important
distinction between Luther and the Anabaptists. This is expressed in the covenantal theology of Pilgram Marpeck, who
drew a sharp distinction between the Old Covenant and the
New.[32] The Christian is called to live in the New Covenant,
not the Old. Therefore he cannot live by the standards of the
Old, or of the world that still lives in the Old. The Anabaptist view of the two kingdoms and their sharp separation
applies not only to one's relationship to the state, but to all
relationships. Christian discipleship involves all of life. The
whole Christian life must be lived under the New Covenant,
separated from the world. He no longer lives by the standards
of the fallen world.

The Anabaptist Value System

The Anabaptists, like most sectarian groups, were seen as
troublemakers more interested in destroying than in building.

---

[30] Quoted by Clarence Bauman, "The Theology of the Two Kingdoms," *Mennonite Quarterly Review*, XXXVIII (January, 1964), p. 41.

[31] *Ibid.*, pp. 42-43.

[32] Jan J. Kiwiet, *Pilgram Marbeck* (Kassel: J. C. Oncken Verlag,
1957), pp. 94-100.

The reason these groups appear so negative, however, is that they have values which they consider so important that they must reject the corruption of the status quo. It was because of radical obedience to Christ and their vision of the kingdom of God that the Anabaptists were forced to reject the dominant values of the sixteenth century. As was noted above, they saw the need for people to live now as if the kingdom of God were already here. This was at the heart of their value system.

The Anabaptists were more interested in living a Christian life than in speculating about it. As Littell has noted,

> ... In contrast to many groups in history and in contemporary Christianity the Anabaptists actually meant what they said. The separation between verbalization and action which has been so marked in contemporary church groups can mislead us in our approach to the Anabaptist movement: the Anabaptists meant just what they said, and their teaching is unimportant apart from the direct attempt to give it embodiment in actual groups living in history.[33]

They saw grace and salvation not as theoretical doctrines, but as something known from personal experience. They were uninterested in theological speculation. As Marpeck stated,

> We recognize as true Christian faith only such a faith through which the Holy Spirit and the love of God came into the heart, and which is active, powerful, and operative in all outward obedience and commanded works.[34]

This is seen in their rejection of sacramentalism (the belief that grace is objectively present in the bread and cup) and other practices. Thus the bread and cup were seen as a "remembrance" of Christ. For the same reason they denied the validity of the Mass and the special office of the clergy.[35] Thus the important word for them was not faith as with Luther, but discipleship (*Nachfolge Christi*).[36] While Luther stood in the Augustinian tradition which emphasized man's

---

[33] Littell, p. 46.

[34] Quoted by Harold S. Bender, "Walking in the Resurrection: The Anabaptist Doctrine of Regeneration and Discipleship," *Mennonite Quarterly Review*, XXXV (April, 1961), p. 101.

[35] Littell, pp. 99-100.

[36] Harold S. Bender, "The Anabaptist Vision," *Recovery of the Anabaptist Vision*, p. 43.

being totally lost in sin, the Anabaptists began with conversion and the new life of the Christian. Rather than focusing on personal salvation, they stressed living in the new kingdom, living by a new set of values (love, peace, forgiveness, etc.). Hans Denck, a South German Anabaptist, stated that "No one can truly know Christ, except he follow Him in life."[37] This meant commitment of one's whole life to Christ.

The Anabaptists had an emphasis on moral purity, as seen in their stress on integrity, noncompromise, and the simple life. The integrity of the Christian life was very important for them. They strongly opposed the forms of religion that did not come from the heart. Menno Simons, the leader of the Anabaptists in Northern Germany and the Netherlands after 1536, illustrates this concern.

> The regenerate, therefore, lead a penitent and new life, for they are renewed in Christ and have received a new heart and Spirit. ... And they live no longer after the old corrupted nature of the first earthly Adam, but after the new upright nature of the new and heavenly Adam, Christ Jesus. ... Hatred and vengeance they do not know. Avarice, pride, unchastity, and pomp they hate and oppose. ... They seek righteousness with all their might. ... In short they are fruit-bearing branches of the true vine.[38]

This life style was affirmed even by their enemies. Franz Agricola, a Roman Catholic theologian, wrote in 1582:

> Among the existing heretical sects there is none which in appearance leads a more modest or pious life than the Anabaptists. As concerns their outward public life they are irreproachable. No lying, deception, swearing, strife, harsh language, no intemperate eating and drinking, no outward personal display, is found among them, but humility, patience, uprightness, neatness, honesty, temperance, straightforwardness in such measure that one would suppose that they had the Holy Spirit of God.[39]

While Luther said that since we live in a sinful world

---

[37] Quoted by Paul Peachey, "The Modern Recovery of the Anabaptist Vision," *Recovery of the Anabaptist Vision*, p. 328.

[38] Quoted by Harold S. Bender, "Walking in the Resurrection: The Anabaptist Doctrine of Regeneration and Discipleship," *Mennonite Quarterly Review*, XXXV (April, 1961), p. 100.

[39] Quoted by Bender, "The Anabaptist Vision," *Recovery of the Anabaptist Vision*, p. 45.

we must compromise with it, the Anabaptists rejected compromise. They felt called to live by the standards of the kingdom, not the standards of this world. Bender describes this
view of the Christian life.

> Since for him no compromise dare be made with evil, the Chris-
> tian may in no circumstance participate in any conduct in the
> existing social order which is contrary to the spirit and teaching
> of Christ and the apostolic practice. He must consequently with-
> draw from the worldly system and create a Christian social order
> within the fellowship of the church brotherhood.[40]

The simple life was also stressed. They urged people to
avoid anything that would lead to pride, and opposed living
on a high economic plane. This was because the New Testament criticized wealth, and because wealth destroys community when one has more than another.[41] Kessler, a contemporary
Reformation leader and chronicler of the Swiss Reformation,
wrote:

> Their conversation and bearing shine forth as entirely pious, holy
> and unpunishable. They avoid ostentatious clothes, despise deli-
> cate food and drink, clothe themselves with coarse cloth, decking
> their heads with broad felt hats, their way and conversation quite
> humble.[42]

They urged their people to refuse to participate in the com-
mercial and financial institutions and were highly critical of
the developing capitalism of that time. In criticism of usury,
Menno wrote: "The whole world is so contaminated and involved with the accursed ... finance, usury, and self interest
that I scarcely know how it could be worse."[43] He listed
among those who "live openly in sin ... all financiers and
bankers, all who love money." Ridemann puts it even more
strongly.

> This only we regard as wrong: when one buyeth a ware and
> selleth the same again even as he bought it, taking to himself

---

[40] *Ibid.*, p. 53.

[41] Donald Sommer, "Peter Ridemann and Menno Simons on Economics," *Mennonite Quarterly Review*, XXVIII (July, 1954), pp.
210-211.

[42] Quoted by Williams, *The Radical Reformation*, pp. 132-133.

[43] Sommer, p. 214.

profit, making the ware dearer thereby for the poor, taking bread from their very mouths, and thus making the poor man nothing but the bondman of the rich. . . . They [the traders] say, however, "But the poor also profit in that one bringeth goods from one hand to another!" There they use poverty as a pretext, seeking all the time their own profit first, and thinking only of the poor as having an occasional penny in their purse.[44]

Freedom was especially important for the Anabaptists, since they struggled so hard and suffered so much for their religious beliefs. Their concept of freedom must be seen from several perspectives. First was their call for separation of church and state, which meant that everyone should have the right to a free, private interpretation of faith within a pluralistic society. No government should have any authority in matters of faith. This was their alternative to the medieval structure. It has been suggested that the Anabaptists were the first to proclaim religious liberty in the way we think of it now.[45] Hans Denck, a South German Anabaptist, illustrates this view of religious freedom.

Such a security will exist, also in outward things, with practice of the true Gospel that each will let the other move and dwell in peace — be he Turk or heathen believing what he will — through and in his land, not submitting to a magistrate [in matters of faith]. Is there anything more to be desired? I stand fast on what the prophet says here. Everyone among all peoples may move around in the name of his God. That is to say, no one shall deprive another — whether heathen or Jew or Christian, but rather allow everyone to move in all territories in the name of his God. So may we benefit in the peace which God gives.[46]

Secondly, freedom meant that the church must be a *voluntary* association of believers. Whoever did join the group was to do so by his own free choice. Thus they had to reject infant baptism, for if Christian faith is to be voluntary, then so must be baptism. The most radical act of the Anabaptists was baptism. Even though adult baptism was punishable by death, they continued to baptize any who would take that step. This was a direct defiance of the system and soon

---

[44] *Ibid.*, pp. 214-215.
[45] Littell, p. 65.
[46] Quoted by Littell, p. 66.

become the symbol of the movement. This was the act that struck to the core of the authoritarian *Corpus Christianum*. It was similar to the burning of a draft card today or the early church's refusal to put a pinch of incense on the fire as a symbol of support for Caesar. Baptism soon became the real issue dividing the establishment men from those seeking a voluntary, believers' church. For Zwingli, the main issue was no longer theological, but political. He wrote: "The issue is not baptism, but revolt, faction, heresy."[47]

For this reason, Paul Peachey can state:

> The Reformers therefore fought the Anabaptists, not because they considered them an immediate revolutionary threat, nor yet because they misunderstood their position, but because the "totalitarian" social order in which they stood and for which they had decided, simply could not tolerate in its midst an autonomous, voluntary, noninclusive social grouping.[48]

We see then that the Anabaptists became early proclaimers of the disestablishment of the church. With the exception of the Hutterite colonies they did not equate the church with the political community. Here we see the beginning of a new era of freedom.

Freedom was based on a profound understanding of community. This meant rejection of the individualism of the Spiritualists, who rejected any church, and of the totalitarianism of the established churches. The Anabaptist vision can never be lived out individually, but must be lived within the context of a group. Friedmann, an Anabaptist scholar, sees this as most important.

> Now then, the central idea of Anabaptism, the real dynamite in the age of Reformation, as I see it, was this, that one cannot find salvation without caring for his brother, that this "brother" actually matters in the personal life.... This interdependence of men gives life and salvation a new meaning. It is not "faith alone" which matters ... but it is brotherhood, this intimate caring for

---

[47] Quoted by Williams, *The Radical Reformation*, p. 131.

[48] Paul Peachey, "Social Background and Social Philosophy of the Swiss Anabaptists, 1525-1540," *Mennonite Quarterly Review*, XXVIII (April, 1954), p. 120.

each other, as it was commanded to the disciples of Christ as the
way to God's kingdom.[49]

Discipleship includes one's brother. Thus they saw the essence of the church to be found within a community of believers. Zschäbitz sees the important fact of Anabaptism in its
coming together in communities outside of the established
church.[50]

Even though they rejected an elaborate system of church
government, they did recognize the need for some type of
organization and leadership. Because of their acceptance of
the priesthood of all believers, they needed no hierarchical
structure. Since the missionary mandate applied to every
Christian, the distinction between laity and clergy almost
disappeared. Littell rightly points out that theologically they
were not self-governing, but insofar as they developed free
discussion for decision making and rejected external political
and ecclesiastical pressures, they developed a democratic form
of government.

> The social scientist may be justified in considering this one of the
> first manifestations of government by consensus. The church his-
> torian finds it one of the first patterns of lay government in Chris-
> tian history, a historical moment when the professional monopoly
> of theologians and canon lawyers was broken in favor of the
> priesthood of all believers.[51]

One could call it the beginning of participatory democracy.

Love was very much at the center of the community. There
was a genuine caring for the neighbor. As Burkholder, a
Mennonite scholar, describes it, "Love was not a mere turning of the cheek from time to time, but the creation of a
continuous network of relationships in which love was in-
trinsic."[52] However, this was not seen as an easy-going senti-
mentalism. It also involved discipline: what they called the

---

[49] Robert Friedmann, "On Mennonite Historiography and on Individualism and Brotherhood," *Mennonite Quarterly Review*, XVIII (April,
1944), p. 121.

[50] Zschäbitz, p. 76.

[51] Littell, p. 94.

[52] J. Lawrence Burkholder, "The Anabaptist Vision of Discipleship,"
Recovery of the Anabaptist Vision, p. 145.

ban. They rejected any other use of compulsion, for they recognized that faith cannot be forced. As Claus Felbinger, a Hutterite, stated in his confession, "God wants no compulsory service. On the contrary, He loves a free, willing heart that serves him with a joyful soul and does what is right joyfully."[53] But since they saw the church as composed of committed Christians, those who strayed from the faith had to be dealt with. For this they used only the threat of loss of privileges within the fellowship and sometimes social ostracism. The Schleitheim Confession recommends the use of the ban, but only after there have been two private confrontations with the offender and one public hearing.[54] Here we see a practice that maintained a disciplined community, and a form of confrontation that had great therapeutic potential for all involved. Peachey sees Anabaptism as "a synthesis between Christian freedom and discipline rare in history."[55]

Free discussion was important for the Anabaptists. Since the Bible was their rule of faith rather than creeds, they depended upon each other for instruction. They were always eager to discuss theological issues with their opponents. This attitude of openness to truth is portrayed by Hubmaier, an early Anabaptist leader.

> I can err, for I am a man, but I cannot be a heretic, for I am willing to be taught better by anybody. And if anyone will teach me better, I acknowledge that I shall owe him great thanks.[56]

This attitude is very much at the heart of their desire to live with others in freedom and is a sound basis for democracy. It should be remembered, however, that their concept of religious liberty was based not on abstract theories of freedom, but on their doctrine of the voluntary church with only Christ as Lord and Master. Staughton Lynd has noted this Anabaptist view of freedom.

---

[53] Robert Friedmann, "Claus Felbinger's Confession of 1560," *Mennonite Quarterly Review*, XXIX (April, 1955), p. 149.

[54] John C. Wenger, "The Schleitheim Confession of Faith," *Mennonite Quarterly Review*, XIX (October, 1945), p. 248.

[55] Paul Peachey, "The Modern Recovery of the Anabaptist Vision," *Recovery of the Anabaptist Vision*, p. 332.

[56] Quoted by Estep, p. 51.

> Few groups have been more devoted to personal freedom than the sixteenth-century Anabaptists, who "when asked their trade and location and station in life in court actions . . . replied, 'No master!' (kein Vorsteer), for in the New Age only Christ was Master."[57]

Their sense of community also had implications for their economic life. This has been noted above in the discussion of the simple life and their rejection of wealth and capitalism. Zschäbitz is right in describing them as rejecting selfish, capitalistic motives.[58] They were early socialists. Each member of the community was considered equal and was expected to share what he had. Spittelmaier's "Seven Decrees of Scripture" illustrates their view of economics.

> Nobody can inherit the kingdom unless he is here poor with Christ, for a Christian has nothing of his own: no place where he can lay his head. A real Christian should not even have enough property on earth to be able to stand on it with one foot. This does not mean that he should go and lie down in the woods and not have a trade or that he should not work, but only that he might not think they are for his own use, and be tempted to say: This house is mine, this field is mine, this money is mine, but rather ours, even as we pray: Our Father. In brief, a Christian should not have anything of his own, but should have all things in common with his brother, not allow him to suffer need. In other words, I do not work that my house may be filled, that my larder be supplied with meat, but rather I see to it that my brother has enough, for a Christian looks more to his brother than to himself (I Cor., ch. 13).[59]

There was no agreement, however, how this ideal should be lived out. For the Hutterites, it meant a structured form of a community of goods with no private property. For most of the other groups it took a voluntaristic form, with a clear teaching of sharing with anyone who was in need. They were all agreed, however, that no Christian should consider his property his own and that he should always respond to the need of his brother as if it were his own need.[60]

---

[57] Staughton Lynd, "Bicameralism from Below," *Liberation*, XII (July, 1967), p. 15.

[58] Zschäbitz, pp. 99-105.

[59] Quoted by Williams, *The Radical Reformation*, p. 173.

[60] Peter James Klassen, "The Economics of Anabaptism, 1525-1560," *Mennonite Quarterly Review*, XXXVII (April, 1963), pp. 131-132.

Important also is their view of man, which contrasts sharply with the mainline reformers. Over against the predestination of Luther and Calvin, the Anabaptists affirmed man's free will and responsibility. They still considered man a sinner, but rejected the view that man is totally depraved, for there can be no discipleship without man's ability to respond. They had an especially deep sense of responsibility to both God and to their fellow man.[61] This is also reflected in their view of salvation, which is seen not as some spiritual effect on man, but a renewal of all of life, for discipleship includes every area of life. It affects both the personal and social dimensions of life. This assumes that through the grace of God man is able to be faithful and to live in the light of the kingdom. In fact, he is commanded to do so.

We must also briefly look at their view of history. In this respect, they were also not pessimistic, but lived in hope. They expected the kingdom to come on earth.[62] This did not mean that they could bring it in themselves, but that they lived with the hope that it was about to come. This is especially important for understanding their whole ethical position. They desired to live by the standards of the kingdom, for they saw the end of history not in the powers of this world, but in the kingdom which was to come.

Strategy for Social Change

One of the significant differences between the Anabaptists and the leaders of the Reformation was the unwillingness of the Anabaptists to work through the magistrates to achieve their goals of reforming the church. This was the point of division between them and Zwingli. Zwingli took a compromising approach, trying gradually to bring his reforms through the establishment. This does not mean, however, that they were narrow-minded separatists. They had tried to work through the structure and bring the established church to change, but soon realized that this was not possible. They then withdrew from the church, but continued to relate to

[61] Williams, p. 863.
[62] Littell, p. 133.

it and call for its reformation. Important for the Anabaptists
was the conviction that the Christian must be different from
the non-Christian. The Hutterite *Article Book* of 1577 states:

> There is a great difference between Christ and the world, like
> that between heaven and earth. World is world and remains al-
> ways world. The Christian, however, is called away from this
> world and is called never to conform to this world. Whoever is
> a friend of this world and is liked by her is no servant of Christ
> who is ever being contradicted on all sides. . . .[63]

We must now consider what this separation from the
world meant for their relation to the establishment. Since they
accepted the authorities as ordained by God, they believed
in obedience to the government. Since they did not distinguish
between a good or bad government, their obedience was independent of the morality of the government. Hans Hillerbrand points out:

> Obedience to the established authorities is an expression of thank-
> fulness to God, who through the appointment of the office of the
> authority declared his kindness. . . . Disobedience to the authorities
> is therefore not only disobedience, but above all also unthankful-
> ness to God.[64]

This obedience, however, related only to those functions of
government that they considered legitimate for the state.
Sattler, during his trial, tried to show that he was a loyal
citizen, that he had not defied the authorities in anything
that was under their jurisdiction.[65] But they were very clear
what that jurisdiction did not include. They first acknowl-
edged the primacy of God's claims over the claims of the
authorities. They considered it more important to obey God
than men. Thus they were ready to disobey any ruling that
conflicted with their beliefs. Claus Felbinger stated in his
confession,

> Therefore we are gladly and willingly subject to the government
> for the Lord's sake, and in all just matters we will in no way

---

[63] Quoted by Robert Friedmann, "The Essence of Anabaptist Faith.
An Essay in Interpretation," *Mennonite Quarterly Review,* XLI (January, 1967), p. 24.

[64] Hillerbrand, *Die politische Ethik. . . ,* pp. 27-28 (my translation).

[65] Bossert, pp. 211-212.

> oppose it. When, however, the government requires of us what
> is contrary to our faith and conscience — as swearing oaths and
> paying hangman's dues or taxes for war — then we do not obey
> its command.[66]

The Anabaptists were also opposed to a Christian holding
public office, although there were various shades of opinion
on this. Erland Waltner, a Mennonite, maintains that Menno
Simons was not as strict as were the Swiss Brethren in sep-
arating the Christian from the state. He states that while the
Swiss Brethren saw the state only as a punitive institution,
Menno believed if the state is administered rightly, it can be
an aid to the kingdom of God.[67] The main reason for ex-
cluding the Christian from public office was because the ethos
of the state conflicted with redemptive love. The *Handbüchlein of 1558*, the Anabaptist answer to Melanchthon, states
that no Christian can take up an office which involves ven-
geance and killing.[68] The Anabaptists saw the use of force
and revenge as inherent in the role of government. Hillerbrand quotes the *Älteste Chronik der Hutterischen Brüder*
in answer to the question whether the state can be Christian.

> If it would deny itself, give up everything, take the cross upon
> itself, rid itself of violence and pomp, and follow Christ, then
> it could be Christian.[69]

Hillerbrand writes that stated negatively this means: "The
state must resist evil and use the sword for punishment. If it
does not do that, then it ceases to be the state."[70] The Schleitheim Confession also opposes participation in government.

> Finally it will be observed that it is not appropriate for a Chris-
> tian to serve as a magistrate because of these points: The gov-
> ernment magistracy is according to the flesh, but the Christians'

---

[66] Quoted by Robert Friedmann, "Claus Felbinger's Confession of
1560," *Mennonite Quarterly Review*, XXIX (April, 1955), p. 147.

[67] Erland Waltner, "The Anabaptist Conception of the Church," *Mennonite Quarterly Review*, XXV (January, 1951), p. 15.

[68] Wilhelm Wiswedel, "The Handbüchlein of 1558," *Mennonite
Quarterly Review*, XXIX (July, 1955), pp. 213-214.

[69] Hillerbrand, p. 47 (my translation).

[70] *Ibid.*

> is according to the Spirit; their citizenship is in this world, but the Christians' citizenship is in heaven. . . .[71]

Thus because they were convinced that the state cannot be Christian, they believed that the Christian should not take part in it. First of all the Christian must be obedient to Christ.

Another aspect of noncooperation with the authorities was their refusal to take an oath. Three main reasons were given. First, it is unnecessary because the Christian is always obligated to tell the truth; second, it was forbidden by Christ; and third, it is impossible because man does not know if he can keep it since he does not control the future.[72] The Schleitheim Confession stated the same position.[73] Another reason may have been the political implications of the oath. In Strasbourg every year the citizens were required to assemble and take the oath of allegiance to the city constitution.[74] It is clear why the Anabaptists refused to follow this directive.

Their position on paying taxes is unclear, since there was disagreement. Some claimed that the authorities have scriptural authority to exact taxes and that the Christian is not responsible for how they are spent.[75] In the *Handbüchlein of 1558*, it is stated that they would pay toll and taxes, but not taxes for war, executions or other injustices.[76] Claus Felbinger in his confession rejects paying hangman's dues or taxes for war, as quoted above. At least we can say that there were those who were selective in what taxes they would agree to pay.

Were the Anabaptists basically anarchists? If everyone were Christian, would there still be a need for government? Felix Mantz is supposed to have said that there should be no government.[77] It could be that they would have seen

---

[71] Quoted by John C. Wenger, "The Schleitheim Confession of Faith," p. 251.

[72] Estep, p. 191.

[73] Wenger, pp. 251-252.

[74] Robert Kreider, "The Anabaptists and the Civil Authorities of Strasbourg, 1525-1555," *Church History*, XXIV (1955), p. 104.

[75] Hillerbrand, pp. 70-73.

[76] Wiswedel, pp. 213-214.

[77] Hillerbrand, p. 9.

Christ as the only authority necessary. Certainly there is an element of anarchism. The question must remain open, however.

We see then that the Anabaptists rejected the notion of bringing change from the top down. They agreed neither with the notion of the state controlling or bringing change into the church, nor with the idea of the church dominating the state. Rather, change must start with communities of believers who live changed lives. Friedmann notes that,

> To the Anabaptists "salvation" (or rather redemption) means the newly-acquired strength to walk the narrow path and to know oneself as a part of the divine drama which will eventually lead to the kingdom of God on earth. It means also the awareness of being a fighter in the incessant warfare between the powers of light and of darkness.[78]

Change comes when people begin to live in the kingdom, and are obedient to Christ. But they went one step farther and said that we can bring in the kingdom neither through institutional forces nor through our own efforts. We must simply begin living in the kingdom. It cannot be forced. For this reason the Anabaptists were dropouts from society, choosing to separate themselves and create their own parallel structures, their own obedient communities where they could live in the kingdom. The real agents of social change were seen as those who accepted the Lordship of Christ and were obedient to him. The community did not live by force, but believed that those who were faithful would be victorious.

Possibly the best-known characteristic of the Anabaptists was their emphasis on nonresistance. They did not believe in the use of force or participation in war. According to Bullinger, the Anabaptists believed that "war is the worst evil that one can conceive."[79] This concept of nonresistance must be seen as coming from their doctrine of the cross, which means a willingness to suffer in the face of evil. Bullinger states:

> They believe that Christians should stand ready to suffer (rather

---

[78] Robert Friedmann, "The Essence of Anabaptist Faith," p. 23.

[79] Quoted by Bender, "The Pacifism of the Sixteenth Century Anabaptists," p. 123.

than strike back).... Christians do not resist violence and do
not take recourse to law.... They do not defend themselves, therefore they do not go to war and are not obedient to the government on this point.[80]

This position should not be confused with modern pacifism,
nor was it basically political. As Littell rightly points out,

For them, pacifism was narrowed to the testimony of the non-
resistant martyrs; the atmosphere was eschatological rather than
utopian, the pattern of behavior one of discipleship rather than
social strategy.[81]

It had its political implications, however. According to Zürich court records, Andreas Castelberger was

... saying much about war; how the divine teaching is so strong
against it and how it is sin. And he expressed the idea that the
soldier who had plenty at home in his fatherly inheritance and
goods and yet went to war, and received money and pay to kill
innocent persons and to take their possessions from people who
had never done him any harm, such a soldier was before Almighty
God, and according to the content of Gospel teaching, a murderer
and not better than one who would murder and steal on account
of his poverty, regardless of the fact that this might not be so
according to human laws, and might not be counted so bad.[82]

A few did advocate the defensive use of the sword, including
Hubmaier, but these were a small minority.[83] In spite of
severe persecution, the Anabaptists were able to maintain this
nonviolent witness. Clemens Adler in a manuscript of 1529
sums up their position.

[They] also have peace with everyone, harm no one in any
respect, neither in body nor in goods, but endure at the hands
of all men all kinds of injustice which may be done to them; yea,
for the love of Christ they love their enemies, do good to them
and pray for them, as Christ teaches them, and thus hearken to
the voice of their shepherd. Even if the world rises up against
them, rages and storms against them, yet they rage and storm
against none; and if the world lifts up its sword against them, yet
they take no sword against it nor against anyone....[84]

---

[80] *Ibid.*

[81] Littell, p. 58.

[82] Bender, p. 122.

[83] *Ibid.*, p. 124.

[84] Quoted by Samuel Geiser, "An Ancient Anabaptist Witness of

Evaluation and Comparison

Because of intensive persecution, the Anabaptists were not able to make the contribution to society that the free churches in England and America could make. We do not know what the effects would have been had Anabaptism been left free to develop and spread. However, in spite of this, Anabaptism has had and is having its impact. The heritage is being kept alive in the Mennonite churches and the Church of the Brethren. But its influence is much broader than this. Bender claims that

> There can be no question but that the great principles of freedom of conscience, separation of church and state, and voluntarism in religion, so basic in American Protestantism, and so essential to democracy, ultimately are derived from the Anabaptists of the Reformation period. . . .[85]

Staughton Lynd believes the "vision of a covenanted community" had an influence on the Declaration of Independence and the American tradition.[86] Williams writes that

> . . . in looking both to the apostolic past and the apocalyptic future, the Radical Reformation induced currents in history and the interpretation thereof . . . ranging from explicitly Christian theologies of history, through democratic progressivism, to Marxism.[87]

Littell points out that

> . . . it has been customary even for many latter-day friends of the movement to assume that the Anabaptists contributed nothing to social and political thought as such. I long thought that study of the contribution of the free churches to democratic development as such must be postponed until the Commonwealth Period in England. However, the implications for a constitutional and just government are also there and some of the direct teachings as well.[88]

There is also evidence to suggest that the Anabaptists had

Nonresistance," *Mennonite Quarterly Review,* XXV (January, 1951), p. 67.

[85] Bender, "The Anabaptist Vision," *Recovery of the Anabaptist Vision,* pp. 29-30.

[86] Lynd, p. 15.

[87] Williams, *Spiritual and Anabaptist Writers,* p. 25.

[88] Franklin Littell, "The Anabaptist Concept of the Church," *Recovery of the Anabaptist Vision,* p. 125.

an impact on the English Puritan Left.[89] More research needs to be done to study the true impact of Anabaptism on our modern world and radical movements in particular. In the meantime, it can be affirmed that the Anabaptists have made a significant contribution.

The premise of this chapter has been that there are many parallels between Anabaptism and the New Left of our own time. The historical backgrounds are similar. Both see society as sick, corrupt, and beyond reform, but at the same time have a profound vision of a new society: what the Anabaptists called the kingdom of God. Their relation to that new society is to live now as if it had already come, and not by the standards of the present world. Life is more important than theoretical or theological speculation, and must be lived out in concrete commitment. The method of witness is not through compromise with the establishment, but rather creating separate communities in order to point to new possibilities and realities. There is an emphasis on community and bonds of love between people. There is hope in man's potential and his ability to be responsible. As the Anabaptists rejected Calvin's predestination, the New Left rejects present forms of determinism. Both have an emphasis on freedom, a concern with voluntarism and participatory democracy. These and many other issues point to the similarities of these two radical stances.

There are also distinct differences. The Anabaptists had a religious basis for their entire position which resulted from obedience to Christ. The New Left is not consciously religious. The Anabaptists stressed that man cannot bring in the kingdom by his own works; he can only live in the light of the revolution that has already taken place in Christ. The New Left, without this eschatological perspective, sees the importance of our building that new society of justice, peace, and love. The Anabaptists had a deep sense of personal sin in addition to their view of the corrupt nature of society. The New Left sees sin as a result of perverted social

---

[89] Bender, "The Anabaptists and Religious Liberty in the 16th Century," p. 85.

structures and does not consider personal origins of sin as a significant factor in society. They do take sin seriously, however.

There is one aspect of Anabaptism of which we need to be critical. Although they were right that we cannot build the kingdom by our own efforts, they did not have a strong enough impulse to witness to the social structures. Although they were very much aware of the evil and oppression that came from the social structures, they failed to realize that we can change social structures even though we cannot build the kingdom. This weakness can best be seen in the present Mennonite-Brethren churches which have tended to withdraw from society and not feel responsibility for it. On their behalf, however, it must be recognized that they did try to relate to the power figures of their day and that witness to the state is made difficult when people are being killed for even disagreeing with it. Their point of view is also a good corrective to the liberal who sees the task of the Christian to order society and build a "Christian" world. Those who today would take the Anabaptist tradition seriously must find ways of combining a forceful witness to the state with the knowledge that the kingdom is not for us to establish. That will be our attempt in the remaining chapters.

Part Two

CHAPTER THREE

Biblical Faith, Radicalism and Hope

The old has passed away, behold, the new has come.
The Apostle Paul

Introduction

To be a Christian is to be a radical. This statement may sound absurd to most people who are acquainted with the church. For many it is more reasonable to consider Christianity as the "opiate of the people," or at best a conservative force which defends the status quo. Although such reasoning is based on sound historical evidence, this does not rule out the revolutionary nature of the Christian faith. The presupposition of this study is that within the Judeo-Christian tradition there is a radical heritage which needs to be recovered and related to our era of turmoil. In spite of what many think, Christian faith does not refer to presidential prayer breakfasts, theologians who justify the status quo, or the local church which opposes open housing.

This study also affirms the need for theology. The protest movement is not based only on negation; it includes affirmation. But when we talk of affirmation, we are already dealing with the theological question of what we shall affirm. On what basis do we affirm what? What is to be the foundation of our values? The assumption being made here is that

79

humanism is not an adequate basis for life. While the affirmations of humanism are important there is a depth beyond the social and empirical realities of life. At the very depths of our own existence there is a future to anticipate, a beyond and unknown which is uncontrollable by man. It seems to be a sociological fact that where there are no gods, men either find them or create them, be they objects, nations, or ideals. Man does search for ultimates. When the Christian names the name of God, he is saying that there is an ultimate beyond our comprehension, and thus nothing finite, no system, no idea, no object may be raised to the level of ultimacy. It is a recognition of a mystery in life that defies all our feeble rationalizations. The Christian also believes that in the person of Jesus of Nazareth we see more than the career of a good man that ended in tragedy and irrelevance. Rather, he finds in the life style of Jesus a revelation of what true manhood is, and something about the nature of ultimate reality. The story of his resurrection points to the transforming impact his life and death had upon those who had followed him. One cannot finally prove in any rational way the validity of the Christian faith. But those who have been grasped by its vision and depth know its power and reality.

The Historical Nature of Christian Faith

One of the important aspects of the biblical world view is its serious consideration of history. Biblical faith is historical faith. The God of the Bible is not a static Greek metaphysical being who is unchangeable and immutable; rather he is the God of history, the God of Abraham, Isaac, and Jacob, a God who reveals himself in historical, political events. The Bible itself was written in the midst of political struggle and repeatedly uses such political metaphors as messiah, kingdom, and justice. History and political events are seen as the sphere of God's activity. The word of God is seen as coming not as ideas, but as events.

This view of God has an important implication for the interpretation of history. History is seen as having purpose and direction, as moving toward a goal rather than being cyclical.[1] It is cumulative rather than repetitive. This view is radically different from either mysticism or Greek idealism. The ancient religions were religions of conformity and the status quo, for man was to adjust himself to Fate. In the biblical view, however, the future is not set and predetermined. God can change his mind about the future if men change their ways (Jer. 18:8, 10). Biblical religion calls men to responsible action in history. The function of God is not to bless what is, but to bring all things under question and judgment. The prophets were concerned with the political and social affairs of the day. Man is seen as a historical being and thus should find his fulfillment within history, rather than through escaping history (mysticism or drugs).

Biblical faith is also secular. It relates to all of life rather than a separate sphere called the sacred. It is just as much concerned with political treaties as with religious ritual. God is seen as Lord over all of life, not only certain parts. This was a most important contribution of the Anabaptists, who were not satisfied with the sacramental religion of their day. The essence of faith is not in salvation rites or mystical union with God, but in the kind of life one lives. The Anabaptists have helped us to recover this aspect of the biblical faith. A vertical relation with God is impossible without a horizontal relation with one's fellow man. The demonic potential of ignoring this aspect of faith can be seen in the person who goes to church and says his little prayers while continuing to oppress and exploit his brother, or in the prayers that were said over the bombs dropped on Hiroshima. When faith is relegated to separate spheres of life, it soon becomes meaningless and absurd or exploitive. True faith deals with life-and-death struggles. Moses called the Israelites to choose between "life and good" and "death and evil" (Deut. 30:15). Camus showed deep insight into Christianity when he wrote that "Christ came to solve two major problems, evil and

---

[1] This is an important aspect of both Christianity and Marxism.

death, which are precisely the problems that preoccupy the rebel."[2] Faith then is inseparable from any area of life.

For faith to be radical, however, it must always be concrete and specific. The word must become flesh. Abstractions are simple enough to accept, but when they become specific they must be dealt with more directly. The more love of mankind becomes general, the more one is able to hate his neighbor. Thus the command to love one's enemy can be repeated in our churches even in war time as long as the enemy is not named. The same can be true for the revolutionary whose revolution, based on the ideals of brotherhood, equality, and freedom, ends in a purge or reign of terror. As one observer put it, "a violent revolutionary is one who loves mankind so much he hates individual people."[3] Christian faith becomes radical when it is combined with commitment and action, not through theological speculation. Faith must become visible and concrete.

Biblical Symbols for Revolution

The Christian church was born in the midst of controversy, for everywhere the Christians went they stirred up trouble through their preaching and teaching, and through their identification with the outcasts and downtrodden. Slaves, thieves, and prostitutes were a prime object of concern. The message was thought of as good news (gospel). A radical change was expected in society, the inbreaking of the kingdom of God. In the Gospel narrative, when Mary had been informed of the birth of Jesus, she responds with these words:

> he has put down the mighty from their thrones,
> and exalted those of low degree;
> he has filled the hungry with good things
> and the rich he has sent empty away.
>   (Luke 1:52-53)

The radical nature of the message was not confined to such proclamations, however. Biblical thought itself has many

---

[2] Albert Camus, *The Rebel* (New York: Alfred A. Knopf, 1954), p. 32.

[3] William R. Faw, "Christian Youth in Rebellion, Resistance, and Revolution," *Signs of the Time* (Elgin, Ill.: Church of the Brethren General Offices, 1967), p. 5.

revolutionary implications. This can be illustrated by examining some of the key concepts of biblical thought.

Creation. The Bible begins with the affirmation that "In the beginning God created heaven and earth." This affirmation was a most significant development in the thought of Israel. Here it is declared that the universe is not controlled by demons and spirits, nor is it divine itself, but rather is created by God and thus subordinate to him. This was the beginning of the freedom of man: the knowledge that he is not controlled by the whims of nature or any other forces around him. It freed man from all domination. Man is to be liberated; not subservient to nature, technology, or the state. As Camus put it, "In a world where things are held sacred the problem of rebellion does not arise."[4] Things are not to be worshiped; they are to be used. Man is given dominion over the earth (Gen. 1:28). With this perspective, man need not be slave to the "elemental spirits of the universe" (Gal. 4:3, 9). The doctrine of creation means that the universe belongs to God, not to Howard Hughes, not to General Motors, not to any state. It belongs to God and is given for all men to use.

Election. The theological beginning of the church was with the calling of Abraham to leave his country and the promise that a great nation would come from his descendants (Gen. 12:1-3). The significance of this election was the call for that nation to be a blessing to all nations. God chose a people, and that people was to exist not for its own purposes but as a blessing to other nations. What a radical turn in political philosophy! A group of people is called to exist for others, a nation is to exist as servant. In this theme of election there is a note of universalism, God's existing for all people. It is the denial of chauvinism and imperialism.

Exodus. The important event for Hebrew faith was the confession that God had delivered the Israelites from slavery in Egypt and brought them to the promised land. Exodus means freedom. The theme of deliverance is an important one for biblical faith and is at the heart of the meaning of

---

[4] *The Rebel,* p. 20.

salvation. It is not a spiritual freeing of the "inner man," but a freeing from political and economic exploitation. It is the deliverance from slavery to freedom, from oppression to peace. Deliverance has been an important word for all oppressed people. It is no accident that the exodus motif has been so central for the Civil Rights Movement. Biblical faith points to liberation wherever there is oppression and exploitation. Jesus came to "preach good news to the poor, to proclaim release to the captives and recovering of sight to the blind, and to set at liberty those who are oppressed..." (Luke 4:18).

Pilgrim People. The people of God are described as pilgrims, sojourners, strangers, and aliens; not as corporation presidents, bureaucrats, or the bourgeois. Abraham was called to leave his home for a strange land; the prophets saw the faithful as a remnant; and Jesus is described as not having a place to lay his head. The Christian is described with the Greek word *xenos* (stranger) in contrast to *polites* (citizen) in Hebrews 11:13. He is a temporary resident, a wanderer, a refugee (I Peter 2:11). *Paroikia* designates a body of aliens in a foreign land and is the root-word for "parish." All this is to say that the church is a set-apart people rather than an institution. They are in the world, but they do not belong to the world (John 17:16). They live by different standards. They are not conformed to this world (Rom. 12:2). A pilgrim people is the very antithesis to an establishment. This is the nature of any revolutionary body. They live by different standards and have different goals than the rest of society. An alien group is a threat to the status quo and always is looked upon with suspicion. The church is called to be this pilgrim group within society.

Judgment. Throughout biblical thought there is the notion that everything is under the judgment of God, that all evil structures stand condemned. This is stated most radically by the prophets, who go so far as to proclaim the destruction of their own nation because of its unfaithfulness. Disobedient structures are to be destroyed, the idols of Baal are to be smashed. The corrupt structures of the world are like the overripe fruit the prophet Amos talked about. Tomorrow they will be rotten. History itself is to be qualified and judged. The prophets called men to act in new ways and not to rely on the securities of the present. If the present order is not ultimate, we have a new freedom to break with the past and begin to face the future in new and creative ways. We are free to attack the sacred nature of the status quo, liberate ourselves from old structures, and point to the new. Jesus acted in this light when he threw the money-changers out of the temple. The role of faith is not to give supernatural sanction to what is, but to call it into question and qualify it, and thus to free the world to fulfill its potential. This means that all present realities are to be qualified, that none are ultimate, and that they will be destroyed if they are idolatrous. Phoney worlds of illusion and pride are to be shattered. All men, all structures (including revolutionaries) come under this judgment. However, also included in this prophetic judgment was the proclamation of a new reality which would follow the destruction.

Messianism. Within ancient Israel there was a tension between the Exodus God, Yahweh, who is a pilgrim God, and the static Baal of agrarian culture, who guarantees the cycles of nature. Israel had to choose between the cyclical view of history found in the fertility cults and in the cycle of seedtime and harvest, and the nomadic religion of migration, direction, and promise. The uniqueness of the biblical view of history is the rejection of historical determinism and thus of traditional society. In biblical thought there is a hope for newness in the future, for society to change, for conditions to become better. The future was expected to break into the present. This undermines a traditionalist view of society where everything is expected to be always the same. This view was expressed most profoundly in the Old Testament hope for the coming Messiah and the New Testament expectation of the kingdom of God. History has not ended, as many bureaucrats would think. Change is still possible, desirable, and necessary. Reality is not static; therefore, it is absurd to adjust oneself to the present, for to do so is to adjust to unreality. The old is passing away and the new is coming.

The Cross. Christian history has been dominated by the cross. Western man has not been able to forget the man who gave up his life that others might find life. In the cross we see the meaning of servanthood, the willingness to suffer for others. The message of the cross is that victory is ultimately to be found not in power and force, but in the midst of defeat and humiliation. God's way of overcoming evil was suffering and defeat on a cross. Although in the eyes of the world the cross is foolishness, in it can be seen ultimate victory. Within a world of power struggles, militarism, and exploitation, the cross stands as a revolutionary reality. Does it make more sense to be servant than master? Is the victory of military might only an illusion? Is suffering more powerful than the infliction of suffering? The cross answers these questions in the affirmative.

Resurrection. The cross ended not in defeat, but in victory. Although we do not know what happened, we know that through what is called the resurrection, defeat was turned into victory, and Jesus was proclaimed as Risen Lord. It is this event that lies at the center of the Christian hope. This victory was described in cosmological terms as the defeat of the principalities and powers. Anyone living in the first century A.D. would have understood what the principalities and powers are. They are the invisible powers that stand behind the powers of this world. It is the power that a small piece of paper (draft card) can have over people's lives. But the early church proclaimed these powers to have been defeated (Colossians 2:10; II Timothy 1:10; I Peter 3:22). The impact of this was to defatalize the world. A person need no longer live in fear and obedience to these powers. Although they have not been annihilated, these powers no longer have control over us. The structures of government, class, toilet training, race, and genes need not determine us. These powers have already been desanctified and delegitimatized. Man is free from them. He can live in freedom. The revolution has already come. Thus man lives in hope; and as any revolutionary knows, hope is an essential part of the revolution.

God as Lord. The proclamation that God is Lord means that Caesar and the President are not. It means that all authorities must be made subject to the one who is Lord of history. It is to proclaim to every government that we have another king (Acts 17:7). Thus the Christian gives to Caesar what belongs to Caesar, and to God what belongs to God. This means he will not give anything to Caesar that does not belong to Caesar. Clearly one's life does not belong to Caesar. Here is a clear disavowal of any totalitarian claims of the state, for the Christian allegiance is not to the state, but to God. Even in Romans 13:1, the most conservative view of the state in the New Testament, it is affirmed that the state exists only by the consent of God and is thus under God. Any authority that claims ultimacy for itself takes on totalitarian and demonic qualities. For this reason the Roman Empire is described in Revelation 13 as the beast which will kill all who refuse to worship it. This is an apt description of a totalitarian state. The Lordship of God means that no finite group can claim ultimacy for itself, for only God is Lord. Thus the Christian cannot pledge allegiance to any institution. The Christian, because of his higher allegiance, is by nature disloyal to all institutions.

Repentance. The biblical message to injustice and sin is repentance. This means to turn around, to go in a different direction. It means to change one's life, not merely to feel sorry for what one is doing. This is the message of the church to the world. If the world is to escape chaos, it must change its unjust ways, it must open itself to new possibilities. The alternative to repentance is destruction. This change must be radical and complete. Halfway measures in regard to our problems will not suffice. We need a total change of attitude and action. Repentance means to stop evil and establish justice. It affirms that change is not only possible, but necessary. The call for repentance points to the possibility of that change.

Conversion. The result of repentance is described as conversion, the new creation, and the new birth. It is the new life that results when one accepts the sovereignty of God. In the words of the prophets, it is the alternative to judgment and destruction. It is that new life called for in the message of repentance. It is that new life lived by the revolutionary in spite of the old order. It is living as if the kingdom had already come. Those who have experienced conversion live in openness to the future by giving shape to the new reality that is coming. This new reality is the life of peace, justice, and hope in the midst of war, injustice, and despair. It is putting the revolution into effect.

Kingdom of God. The biblical metaphor for the end of history is the political term, kingdom of God. It is the time when God will truly be Lord, when the defeated principalities and powers will finally be shown for what they really are. It is the expectation of something new in history. It is not something we achieve, not the religious term for the spiritual achievements of culture, but rather something new, which breaks in at special points in history through events pregnant with new possibilities. It cannot be identified with any present political or social order. The kingdom is that final revolution toward which all the faithful look. It is that time when swords will be beaten into plowshares (Isaiah 2:4), when the mighty will be put down and the lowly lifted up (Luke 1:52), and all tears shall be wiped away (Revelation 21:4). It is that time when peace and love will be the norm. The kingdom is the standard by which the Christian lives. Since he knows that the revolution is coming, and in fact has already made itself known, he lives by its standards rather than the standards of the fallen world. It is this vision of the kingdom that is the hope of the revolutionary.

The Doctrine of Sin

At the heart of radicalism is the concept of sin. The radical rejects a rosy, Pollyanna view of the world. Rather he sees alienation, injustice, and oppression which need to be overcome. Without the concept of sin, there would be little need to seek change. Both biblical and Marxist faith see the structures of society as fallen and the struggle between good and evil as being important. Both also envision the ultimate victory of justice over injustice. Important for biblical thought is the concept of the fall, that man is not what he was meant to be or could be. Thus in spite of modern theories of evolution, the story of Adam and Eve and their expulsion from the garden can speak with meaning. Man is still aware of this fall both in his own life and in the society around him.

Little needs to be said here about the depth of evil in our society. The New Left analysis of society described in Chapter One very adequately depicts the corrupt nature of our social institutions. However, sin and alienation relate to more than social structures, for they also describe the condition of man. It is man who built those oppressive structures, who continues to exploit his brother. With all the inhumanity and degradation of the twentieth century, it would be difficult to ignore the great evil potential of man. It is too simple to blame all alienation on the effect of society upon us. Man rebels against God and his brother and finds himself estranged even from his own self. We also have little basis for believing that man can save himself, that he can take hold of his condition and overcome his alienation. One of the weaknesses of liberalism is that it fails to take evil seriously enough. There is less chance for disillusionment if we have no illusions about man. We should not base our hope on the goodness of man. However, we also dare not use the sin of man to justify capitalist society on the basis that man is selfish or that change is impossible. As will be seen below, however, the sin of man is not the basis for action.

It is especially important for the radical to have a personal view of sin, since one of the common pitfalls for the radical is pride and self-righteousness. It is easy for us to see all evil as existing in structures outside of ourselves without realizing that we also participate in that evil. We must go beyond the TV-western view of man — the good guys against the bad guys. Rather all men are capable of great evil and great good. We must always realize that we also participate in the evil we condemn, that when we judge our nation we also judge ourselves. The prophet speaks with anger, but also with sorrow, for he is a part of his judgment. The failure to keep this in mind can lead to an elitist approach to reform where the good guys lord it over the bad guys. The democratic approach is to see everyone as participating in alienation. Could we call it "participatory sin"?

The Christian Hope

Radicalism not only takes alienation seriously, but also lives with the vision that things can be changed, that things need not be the way they are now. The radical believes in salvation; he has hope. He is able to live in hope in spite of present frustration. Rebellion itself comes out of faith rather than the absurd. Crane Brinton points out that revolutions do not originate with the oppressed, starving, and downtrodden peoples but with the discontented, relatively more prosperous people.[5] Revolutions originate in hope, not despair. James C. Davies points out that in places of starvation, the main concern is with staying alive. Under situations of impoverishment, bad conditions are patiently endured.[6] Revolution becomes a possibility only when people begin to see hope, when they have a vision of a liberated community. How one views the "not yet" is an important factor in how one lives in the present. The present is viewed in terms of the future.

This analysis of revolution points to the radical nature of Christian faith, for while biblical thought has a realistic view of man's predicament it has an eschatological hope that transcends all defeat and despair. The Christian message is about the future of man, a future that has already come in Christ. As was noted above, the Christian looks forward to a new reality which will break into history, a new reality which in fact has already come. The revolution has already occurred in Christ, a revolution that has not yet been completed, but

---

[5] Crane Brinton, *The Anatomy of Revolution* (New York: Prentice-Hall, 1952), p. 278.

[6] James C. Davies, "Toward a Theory of Revolution," *American Sociological Review*, XXVII (February, 1962), p. 6.

will be completed in the end time. This new reality is called the kingdom of God. It is the expectation that society will be changed, that the old will pass away and the new will come. It is the faith that ultimately God will triumph over the forces of evil. It is the realization that a new era has already invaded history and will eventually come to fulfillment. The eschatological vision in the book of Revelation is that the collision of the two worlds of good and evil has already occurred, and that God has already been shown victorious. The world has been shown for what it is. This attitude was contained in an invitation to a New Year's Eve party sponsored by the Chicago Area Draft Resisters (CADRE) in December, 1967. The invitation called for a celebration of the end of the war and the abolishment of the draft, even though those were the two big problems they were fighting. This is the nature of hope. Thus the Christian lives in the faith that the kingdom has already been shown to us, is continuing to break in upon us, and will soon come to fulfillment.

Some may see this as an escapist ideology. It is in fact just the opposite. It is not comfort for enduring distress and pain in life. Rather it is the basis of a radicalism that cannot be crushed by any opposition. It is the rejection of the phrase, "That's the way the cookie crumbles" and the affirmation that the cookie indeed does not need to crumble that way. It is the affirmation that one need not be defined by the present situation, that he can live on the basis of new possibilities, that he can no longer be controlled by the socioeconomic forces around him. He is free to act in new ways. Hope frees one from becoming reconciled to the present. Because of his anticipation of the future, he need not cling to the past or defend the status quo.

The new theology of promise and hope has reminded us that God should not be thought of as being "up there," or "in here," or "between persons," but rather as "the one who goes before us." Our eyes should be focused on the pillar of fire rather than looking back to Egypt. Since God is a God not only of the past but also of the future, one can be open to radical change. Because of his vision of a new era, of a new humanity, one becomes free for others, free to create new alternatives. To live a different kind of life becomes a real possibility. He no longer needs to live by the conservative ethic of self-interest. He now has the freedom not to be primarily concerned about his own piece of property, or his future, but to be receptive to the changes that may come about. In contrast to bourgeois religion, Christian radicalism has a sense of urgency and anticipation. If the new era is coming, it is important that one be prepared for it, that one begin to live already in its promise.[7]

The radical implications of hope can be seen in Marxism's vision of the coming new humanity. Marxism, like Christianity, is profoundly eschatological. The Christian expects a new era to replace this old age. In a quite similar way the Marxist looks forward to that revolution which will completely replace the old order and begin the creation of a new society and a new man. It is indeed unfortunate that the political stance of Western nations (and the church) has created an image of Christianity as being conservative and counterrevolutionary. The proclamation of a new society should not be left to the Marxists, for the Christian has a vision that is even more radical. Yet Marxism stands almost alone in the proclamation of its eschatological hope, while the even more revolutionary hope of Christianity is stifled and undercut by its adherents. Christians should be in the fore in their proclamation of revolution and hope.

When one sees ultimate reality as promise for the future, there is the realization that the center of history does not rest in governments and bureaucracies. The present power centers are not considered determinative for the future. In the eyes of those who have hope, these oppressive powers no longer have their grip on man. With hope for the future, men are freed from slavery to these structures. When the oppressed people of the world catch a new vision of what could be, they will no longer be as easily held down. Chris-

---

[7] For an excellent discussion of the meaning of hope, see Jürgen Moltmann, *The Theology of Hope* (New York: Harper and Row, 1967).

tians should be proclaiming this hope to those who are oppressed.

When we deal with hope, we must also consider unbelief and despair. Unbelief is grounded in hopelessness and a lack of faith. Sin is helplessness, inertia, resignation, and apathy. Though man has been given life and freedom, he despairs and retreats; though the promise of new life has been given, man acts as if the old is eternal; though man has been given potential, he refuses to believe that he is able. This is sin. Hopelessness can take two forms. It can be despair and surrender, or it can result in the fanaticism of demanding complete fulfillment for oneself with no regard for others. The one who loses hope either demands immediate fulfillment or expects nothing at all. Either way, he lives without a promise for the future.

Hope means a rejection of nihilism and hedonism. Love is almost impossible without hope for the future, for if the present is all that one has, the happiness and pleasure of the present become ultimate. There is a connection between despair and egoism. But because of hope, one is freed to participate in the suffering of one's brother and to take responsibility. Some would argue that hope denies fulfillment in the present. Rather, the believer is the one who truly lives in the present with all its possibilities. He is the one who can affirm the joy of the present and face the future unafraid. He lives in hope.

CHAPTER FOUR

Compromise, Expediency and Obedience to Christ

> *Mediocrity has slain its thousands,*
> *but compromise its ten thousands.*
> Norman MacFarlane[1]

Introduction

To be a Christian is to be an extremist. Moderation is a Greek ideal, not Christian. Christian faith is not a halfway measure; it talks about going two miles instead of one, of plucking out eyes that disturb, of dying on a cross. It is to risk death, to love enemies, and to pray without ceasing. As one biblical writer put it, "Would that you were hot or cold! So because you are lukewarm, and neither cold nor hot, I will spew you out of my mouth" (Revelation 3:15-16). Terrence Eagleton of the British New Left has written, "... Christianity is an extremist belief, extreme and uncompromising in its tolerance and love."[2] The Christian is not satisfied with maintaining a tension between the good and the possi-

---

[1] Norman MacFarlane, "Navy Chaplaincy: Muzzled Ministry," *The Christian Century*, LXXXIII (November 2, 1966), p. 1338.

[2] Terrence Eagleton, *The New Left Church* (Baltimore: Helicon Press, 1966), p. 2.

ble. He does the good regardless of consequences or effectiveness. Faith involves intensity and commitment. We are called to love God with our whole being. Radicalism believes that it has something unique to offer that stands over against the other options.

The Problems of Compromise

Most Christians consider compromise to be a necessary and important part of the Christian ethic. Since life can never be unambiguous, it is reasoned that compromise is the only "reasonable" way of relating to the complexities of society. One must simply be "realistic" about how the biblical message is to be followed. Out of the sectarian tradition as evidenced by Anabaptism, however, has come a rejection of compromise and expedience, and a stress on obedience and discipleship. Today the question of compromise is being raised not only by sectarian religious groups, but also by the young protest movement as it rejects the liberal options (including compromise). Within Christendom, also, there can be found the rise of a new Christian radicalism, which among other things is reevaluating the question of compromise and obedience. Both the political and religious radical reject compromise and see it as basically a sell-out.

The purpose here is not to ignore that life is always ambiguous, or that life is impossible without compromise. It is not even to deny the impossibility of living with another person without a degree of compromise. But it is one thing to talk of compromise in the sense of flexibility and cooperation, a willingness to live with the ambiguities of life, to be aware of our questionable motives and imperfect actions, to reject dogmatism; and it is quite another thing to talk of selling out, retreating, being less than faithful, basing decisions on expediency rather than on faithfulness to one's commitment. It is this second kind of compromise that is rejected by the radical and that is the subject of our study. This type of compromise can most often be seen in the division of personal and social ethics, choosing the lesser of two evils, and using the ends to justify the means.

One classical way the church has dealt with the problem of compromise is through the doctrine of the two kingdoms. With this doctrine Luther could maintain a distinction between personal and social ethics. This split between the personal and the social has been one of the biggest tragedies of Western ethics. We have assumed different expectations of people in institutional roles than we have of them in personal relationships. This dichotomy must be overcome. Because of this split between personal and social morality, individuals will do things in the context of an institution or bureaucracy that they would never do as individuals. Because most people have accepted the dictum that institutional morality is different, we have tolerated and even condoned the worst of atrocities. It is at least questionable whether former President Johnson would have been willing to take children in his back yard and burn them with napalm, yet he gave the orders that were responsible for napalming thousands of children to death in Vietnam. On the basis of this ethic, "respectable" American youth can burn down the villages of Vietnam, an Eichmann can plead innocence because he was "only following orders," and theologians can justify moral man accepting the realities of immoral society. Because of this split we reason that certain acts committed by societies and institutions are not as evil as the same acts committed by individuals. As Paul Furfey has so well put it,

> It is an infinitely tragic fact that the greatest crimes of history are committed with the cooperation or at least with the passive consent of the solid citizens who constitute the stable backbone of the community. The sporadic crimes that soil the front pages, the daily robberies, assaults, rapes, and murders are the work of individuals and small gangs. They are committed by manifest criminals whom the community despises and punishes. But the great evils, the persecutions, the unjust wars of conquest, the mass slaughters of the innocent, the exploitations of whole social classes — these crimes are committed by the organized community under the leadership of respectable citizens.[3]

The church has reinforced this view through relegating

---

[3] Paul Hanly Furfey, *The Respectable Murderers: Social Evil and Christian Conscience* (New York: Herder and Herder, 1966), p. 17.

the gospel to private and interpersonal relationships. This has fit well with the development of capitalism. Modern industrial society considers the role of religion to be in the subjective, personal, and individualistic aspects of life. It is careful to keep religion out of those areas which would be threatened by the Christian perspective. It sees faith as having no significance for social and bureaucratic relationships. Thus God is not the God of society, the world, or history. He becomes a privatized idol. Justice, righteousness, and truth become void for most of man's experience. Even the concept "neighbor" is considered unimportant except in personal encounter. Most churches have concerned themselves only with changing men's hearts, forgetting that one cannot separate the person from his social relationships. Other more "liberal" churches have spoken to social problems, but still have maintained a different standard of morality for society than for individuals. Churches that preach against murder applaud their sons for duty in the military!

In developing a social ethic, it must be recognized that there are no relationships that have not been institutionally structured and there are no institutional relationships that do not involve persons. The two cannot be separated. Every decision made in a bureaucratic context affects people, and should be thought of in the same way as an individual action that affects people. Both must be judged by the same norm. Institutions and groups, like individuals, have a centeredness and personality. The decision-making process for both involves the same kind of ambiguities of choice. The argument that groups must operate by consensus is no argument for a different ethic when one realizes that the individual is likewise torn in opposite directions when faced with a choice. Neither individuals nor institutions can be considered responsible and still remain noncommital on important moral issues. Neither should be given the license to transcend the life-death decisions by remaining neutral in time of crisis. For either individuals or institutions to remain silent in the face of injustice is to participate in that injustice and to be responsible for it. Since both have a corporateness and centeredness, both should be expected to operate by the same moral standards. This applies both to the institution as a corporate body in its decision making and to the individual as he makes decisions within his institutional roles. Thus the individual must be held responsible for all decisions he makes within the institution. The President and the American soldiers must be held responsible for the death of so many Vietnamese people. There may be no appeal to "only having followed orders."

It may be argued that this is impossible for many institutions, either because they could find no consensus within their structures, or because taking a stand would mean their demise. This may be true. But if it is true, then it is all the more important for the Christian (or anyone else) to call that institution into question and advocate its transformation or possibly even its elimination. At least people should refuse to cooperate with it. This kind of action has been best demonstrated by student protest against corporations that manufacture napalm and other instruments of death used in Vietnam. Their representatives and their factories have been confronted with the murder they are participating in.

It is important then that the same witness be made to social institutions as to individuals. We must affirm that nations and institutions, like individuals, must be moral, and that when they are not, decay and death are certain. When nations cease to be moral, their demise has already begun. Theologically this is described as the judgment of God. This means that God turns evil structures against themselves. It is what Marx meant when he talked of the inherent contradictions of capitalism. The task of the Christian is to remind the state of its tenuous existence.

In the Christian witness to the state, the state must be called to do more than just live up to its own ideals. It must be recognized that the state stands under the same demands and judgments as does the individual, and thus should be called to live by the same ethics as the individual. It must be proclaimed to the state that if it fails to live under God, if it claims ultimacy for itself, or if it treats others unjustly, it has in reality sown the seeds of its own destruction. Whenever the state lives by killing, oppression, or exploitation, it has begun its own downfall. *If we believe that in the life style of Jesus is to be seen the definition of reality and sanity, then a nation that lives by domination, violence, and coercion is going the way of unreality and ruin.* Christian witness must remind the state of this reality. The Christian should do more than just call the state to live by its own standards.

At the heart of the rationale for compromise is the belief that when faced with two undesirable choices, one should choose the one that is less evil. It is doing less than what is best because of the circumstances. It is a compromise of the ideal when one is convinced that a present danger or opportunity demands a temporary detour from final goals. Although with some uneasiness, Western civilization has accepted this as a valid ethical stance. This rationale for compromise has come under increasing attack in recent years, however, through the rise of new radical and sectarian movements. It is seen as basically an establishment rationale used to justify the status quo. Ernst Troeltsch has noted that the attitude toward compromise is one of the important distinctions between the establishment and radical mentalities.[4]

Choosing the lesser of two evils must be rejected for various reasons. First it means choosing between alternatives set up by someone else rather than presenting an alternative of one's own; it is really no choice at all, since choice in this case is only a passive act. We need to be rejecting the current options and instead creating new alternatives.

A more serious problem with this approach is that it assumes that there are only two possible choices (or at least a limited number of choices), an assumption that is always dangerous to make since it severely limits one's potential actions. One should never assume that there are only two possibilities of action. One should always be open to an unlimited number of alternatives. Thus it is not necessary to choose the lesser of two evils, for it is possible to choose

[4] Benjamin A. Reist, *Toward a Theology of Involvement: The Thought of Ernst Troeltsch* (Philadelphia: Westminster Press, 1966), pp. 156-163.

what is right. It may mean creating a third alternative, refusing to cooperate, or it may mean the cross; but the choice is there.

Another serious problem with choosing the lesser evil is that it justifies an evil act on the basis of the existence of evil, saying that the existence of evil justifies more evil. It is to support an evil alternative only on the basis of evil. The implications of this kind of logic are clear. It is the basis for the absurd reasoning that although America should never have gotten involved in Vietnam and although we are wrong in being there, still since we are there we need to stay there. This argument uses the evil of the status quo as the basis for supporting the status quo. It is the argument that since evil is unavoidable, we should "sin bravely." Barbara Brandt illustrates the tragedy of this position when she describes the person who decides to work within the system.

> Where he has gone wrong is that in his own thinking and acting he has not gone beyond the way things are now. The system says that money and power are important and that you have to be ruthless and efficient to get hold of money and power. Just like the compromiser, he has forgotten the *people* he is working for, and their basic desires. Instead he lets the values and structures of the *system* determine what he does. He cannot bring about any changes in the way things are, because instead of working to build something new, he is all caught up in *reacting* to the system.[5]

There is little hope for positive action to come out of decisions that are justified on the basis of an outmoded, fallen world. As will be explored in the next chapter, the alternative to this approach must be to point to a new way. It is not the task of the Christian to adjust himself to the fallen world.

The plague of this position becomes even more clear when we realize that compromise and expediency can easily become a rationalization for what we really want to do, rather than what we should do. It can in fact become a justification for most anything. We can rationalize killing hundreds of thou-

---

[5] Barbara Brandt, "Why People Become Corrupt," *The New Radicals*, ed. Paul Jacobs and Saul Landau (New York: Vintage Books, 1966), p. 129.

sands of Vietnamese people because we are told in effect that this is a lesser evil than allowing them to become communist. When one goes down this road, morality and truth are no longer considered relevant to the political scene. Expediency becomes the final norm.

At best, compromise is a watering down of one's position. Often it means a direct sell-out. When one weakens his position to make it more acceptable, he has not strengthened it. When an idealist runs for political office and denies his own position in order to become elected, he has in effect sold out his values and betrayed the people he has appealed to. When one's concern is to make his view acceptable, he has already sold out. As Bonhoeffer put it, "... Where the question of relevance becomes the *theme of theology,* we can be certain that the cause has already been betrayed and sold out."[6] Even Troeltsch, who considered compromise an important principle, wrote shortly before his death,

> It is true, however, that in the use of compromise we have to guard against all precipitate capitulation to the course which presents itself as momentarily expedient, or as the easiest way out of a difficulty, but which may be thus expedient and easy only for the moment, and, once more, we have to guard against any fundamental abandonment of the ideal.[7]

This recognizes the radical's concern. Those who would advocate compromise must show by what means they will seek to avoid this sell-out. How sad it is when people build bridges without having anything to carry across them after they are finished.

Some will argue that one's decision must be based on a "realistic" assessment of the facts. Political realism has been the basis for most social decision making. Politics has been defined as the "art of compromise." But how unimpressive the history of this "art" has been! What has been termed practical has in reality failed to be very practical. Partly due to the policy of "realistic" strategists, we find ourselves faced with the present international and domestic crises. It has

---

[6] Dietrich Bonhoeffer, *No Rusty Swords* (New York: Harper and Row, 1965), pp. 309-310.

[7] Reist, p. 168.

proven extremely naive to assume that one can base a decision on what the consequences of that decision will be, since it is impossible to know what the results of our actions will be. To base decisions on the context assumes one can know the entire context of the decision. The truth is, however, that we can never have a very clear perspective on where we are in history. This is especially true also for high officials in bureaucratic structures, for they cannot see the consequences of their actions. How can one calculate consequences in the face of so many unknown variables? How can we predict the consequences of our actions? The experienced diplomat George F. Kennan has affirmed this impossibility.

> I can testify from personal experience that not only can one never know, when one takes a far-reaching decision in foreign policy, precisely what the consequences are going to be, but almost never do these consequences fully coincide with what one intended or expected. This does not absolve the statesman of his responsibility for trying to find the measures most suitable to his purpose, but it does mean that he is best off when guided by firm and sound principle instead of depending exclusively on his own farsightedness and powers of calculation.[8]

The philosophy of "realism" is inadequate. "Expediency" has not proven to be very expedient.

A third popular justification for participating in evil is that the ends justify the means. This argument asserts that one may use most any kind of means, providing that the objective is a good one. Therefore no methods or actions can be ruled out without knowing the purpose for which they are being used. Although a certain action could never be accepted on its own merits, given the proper context it is considered acceptable. We must be prepared to use "any means necessary," we are told.

This assertion is based on the presupposition that it is possible to separate the means from the ends. A more realistic appraisal would tell us, however, that in fact they cannot be distinguished, for they are identical. If the ends we seek are

---

[8] George F. Kennan, "Foreign Policy and Christian Conscience," *The Atlantic,* CCIII (May, 1959), p. 44.

not a part of the means, how is it possible to achieve the desired ends? The desired end must be present in the means or it cannot be reached. Likewise, the evil means will be a part of the end, for if the evil means are used, how will they be separated from the end? Certainly the end cannot be reached in the abstract. It is organically connected with the means. The means used to achieve future goals are more significant to the future than is the nature of the intended goals. By this time we should have learned from history that evil means do not produce good ends. Democracy, for example, cannot be created by nondemocratic means of change. Berdyaev illustrated this insight.

> The good ends of the French Revolution, liberty, equality and fraternity, were also achieved by violence and terror which raged throughout the Revolution. And the result was the capitalist system of the XIX century, in which there was no equality and even less fraternity. The Russian communist revolution also employed terror, and up to now it has created neither brotherhood nor a communal society. Freedom is never achieved by violence, brotherhood through hatred, peace by bloody conflict. Evil means are poisonous. The autumn of revolution never resembles its spring. ... When hate and revenge are invoked for the sake of liberation, enslavement is the result.[9]

If the means are to be justified by the ends, then the only way that the means are truly justified is if the end is actually achieved. If not, we have been deceived by another lie of history. How often people have been duped into going to war to achieve some great purpose such as ending all wars. One more blood bath, we are told, and then there will be peace and justice. There will be much less chance for deception if the end is already apparent in the means one is called to use. In this case victory is not as imperative, for even if the result is defeat, one has already participated in the good end.

In our modern world this fuzzy thinking about ends and means has led us to a possibly even more serious crisis. Jacques Ellul sees that for modern man everything has be-

---

[9] Nicolas Berdyaev, *The Realm of Spirit and the Realm of Caesar* (New York: Harper & Brothers, 1952), pp. 88-89.

come means.[10] The end is no longer significant. The means justify themselves. If something is efficient, it is justified. If it succeeds, it is good; if it fails it is bad. We do not ask, Efficient for what? Good for what? For what purpose is our technology? More technology? We applaud breaking speed records because they are broken. The corollary of this is that man also becomes a means, since things are not subservient to him. Man is a means for the corporation, for the labor union, for the state. He is a producer, a consumer, a citizen. All things become neutral. There is no distinction between good and bad. Chairs, bombs, concentration camps, all are neutral. We have nothing to qualify these creations. How does one argue with moon rockets, miracle drugs, and computers? We are told that they have to be accepted. The point is that we have sacrificed the ends for the sake of the means.

Obedience to Christ as the Answer

When one rejects compromise, there is the assumption that one holds to some kind of ethic that is central and should not be compromised. But immediately one is faced with the question of what the basis is for one's uncompromising stand. By what is this stand to be qualified? What is the norm for action? The very premise of radicalism is that there is an *ought* standing over against the *is*. The radical is one who is not satisfied with the way things are.

The question of what one is to be faithful to is most significant. If one does not have a firm basis for decision making, he is likely to be driven by his environment rather than respond creatively to it. The norm for what ought to be dare not be the way things are now. This is conservatism, a view that wants to be judged only by the status quo. Obviously the radical will not want to operate on the values of his opponents. The radical cannot accept the relativist position that there is no right position, that all positions are equally valid. We must not submit to being judged by history or historical determinism. What *should be* must not be de-

---

[10] Jacques Ellul, *The Presence of the Kingdom* (New York: Seabury Press, 1967), pp. 62-72.

termined by what history produces. History leads to concentration camps, genocide and nationalistic oppression. A revolutionary is one who stands against the tide of history. The events of history need not be accepted as good just because they took place. The radical must decide what he will accept and what he will reject in history.

Just as one cannot allow what *is* to be the norm, so also we must reject absolute principles. Authority should not be based on a call to individual conscience, the German race, the American way of life, the voice of the people, or even majority rule. Abstractions of this kind have too much demonic potential if allowed to become absolute. In fact, the worst atrocities in history have been committed in the name of lofty principles. Crusades, religious wars, and inquisitions are based on principle.

One of the very real dangers in taking a radical or extremist position is that one can very easily become a fanatic, or become totalitarian in one's perspective. This is not to call for moderation, but to point out the need for any movement to be able to criticize itself. Any ideology or movement must have something beyond itself to qualify it. This is perhaps the most serious weakness in Marxism. Although Marx understood the horizontal dialectic, he refused to recognize the vertical dialectic between the finite and the infinite, between the conditional and unconditional. Marxism is profound in its critique of bourgeois culture, but has proven unable to direct that same criticism against itself. Therefore it has no defense against totalitarianism. The tragedy of revolutionary movements is that although they come from a prophetic message, they fail to apply this same judgment against themselves. Because the vertical dimension is lost, there is nothing higher than the party.

The Christian alternative to this problem is transcendence. This means that finally God cannot be identified with any group, nation, or ideology, for he stands in judgment over all of them. Since only God is ultimate, nothing finite may be raised to ultimacy (idolatry). Tillich calls this the Protestant principle.[11] Tillich saw the importance of Protestantism in that it could transcend its own form and never be wholly identified with any concrete form. It holds that every expression of religion and culture must be looked at critically. It affirms that only God can be given absolute allegiance. It means to recognize that there is always a difference between the potential and what exists. The future always escapes the present, and what might be is never the same as what is. This is to recognize that *what is* is not the kingdom of God. Radicalism must keep this in mind, for when it can no longer criticize itself, it becomes reactionary conservatism (e.g., Stalin), trying to defend what it has already established. *Transcendence may never mean justification of what we do, but only judgment and qualification of our action.* Those who use religion to support the status quo do not understand the nature of Christian faith.

For radical Christianity the answer is obedience to Christ. The Christian sees in the life and death of the man Jesus of Nazareth a life style that illuminates the true meaning of life and reality. His is the life that still speaks to us with power and puts our world and our lives under judgment. He was the man who lived for others, who met evil with suffering love, and was willing to die that others might live. He is not to be seen as a demigod, but rather as the birth of promise, expectation, and hope. He is the one who through history has been impinging on man and society. In themselves discipleship and obedience are very ambiguous terms, but when qualified by the life and teachings of Jesus they become specific and concrete. It is very important that the radical vision always be concrete and avoid utopian dreaming or mystical illusion. The vision must be concrete. That is why Jesus is so important.

For Christian faith the norm is not a principle but a person. An important part of biblical faith (although most of Christian history has denied it) is that truth is relational and personal rather than propositional. Persons are more im-

---

[11] Paul Tillich, *The Protestant Era* (Chicago: University of Chicago Press, 1948), pp. 162-163.

portant than principles since Christ died for people, not principles. Truth is relational, for God is dynamic rather than static. Therefore truth is not something that flows through history unaffected by historical events. Truth is always related to historical realities, but never judged by them.

Discipleship is not legalism. It is not holding on to absolute truths or unchangeable principles. Obedience to Christ means a rejection both of absolutism, which has eternal truths unrelated to life, and of contextualism, which ends in no norm except the context. In either case one becomes irrelevant. Rather it is a complete life lived in obedience to our best understanding of reality, namely Jesus the Christ. The real legalism comes when one begins making decisions based on calculations of consequences and practicality. Ellul has pointed out that modern man has been dominated by facts. He is not allowed to question modern technology lest he be accused of wanting to return to a cave.

> . . . These are no longer the questions which man, "because he knows good and evil," can raise about the very existence of the atomic bomb, about the existence of a fact. Thus man divests himself of his true dignity, and he who should dominate things and the world becomes the slave of "facts"; this "slavery" is more complete than any intellectual dictatorship ever hoped to achieve.[12]

The real legalism is based on facts and principles. Christian faith is rooted in a person and thus relationship is more important than fact. Commonly assumed facts can be questioned.

It may sound paradoxical to state that it is in obedience to Christ that one finds true freedom. This, however, is the Christian claim, for it is the call truly to live in freedom and responsibility. Obedience to Christ frees one from all slavery to human institutions and expectations. It is a radical freedom from the tyranny of death, possessions, and success. It is the freedom *to be* in spite of the denial of freedom. True freedom lies not in irresponsibility, but in the knowledge that we are truly free to live for our neighbor. It frees one from the paralyzing consideration of self-interest. To be obedient to the

---

[12] Ellul, p. 39.

command not to commit adultery, for example, frees one from the fear that the other may be unfaithful and increases the freedom to give oneself to the other in love and confidence. One acts responsibly in family, friendship, and society not because of a "thou shalt not," but because of an awareness of the presence of God in those relationships. The prohibition of adultery is not the center of marriage; rather it is the recognition of the presence of the holy in that relationship.

Obedience to Christ means that one does not make decisions on the basis of consequences, expediency, or effectiveness. It means that one does what is right regardless of the result. The radical dares to risk failure. It is not wrong to ask the question of whether one's action will be effective, but it is wrong to use effectiveness as the criterion for action. The important question to ask is, Is it right? Socrates, before he drank the hemlock, did not first ask if Plato would write about him. In fact, it is demonic to act as if one's action will be immortal. Thus one should neither retreat if defeated nor fall into pride and abuse of power if one should succeed. One should not calculate whether his action will be considered respectable and acceptable. Success or failure is not the issue. It is more important to be faithful than to be effective.

In our pragmatic society, the temptation is to equate success with goodness. If it works, it must be good, we are told. This is the necessary conclusion of pragmatism, for it makes part of the action (result) the basis of judging the action. Thus any transcendence is denied. For the Christian, however, ethics are based on the kingdom rather than on society. Just because something is successful is no reason for accepting it. Even if the United States were to achieve a military victory in Vietnam, that would not in any way justify that action.

This ethic does not imply that one should act irresponsibly or hope that one will be unsuccessful. It does not mean that consequences should not be considered. The point is that decisions are not to be made on the basis of the consequences; the consequences are not the judge. One always hopes for success, but failure to predict success does not mean a certain action should not be taken. The draft resister hopes he will escape prison, but because he sees his action as necessary and right he is willing to accept the consequence of his action. This attitude is especially important in a time of repression. Threats of arrest and persecution must not be allowed to intimidate the Peace Movement or stifle dissent. It is imperative that radicals act on what is right, rather than what is expedient.

This also does not mean that one should not be political in his action. Obedience does not mean to choose the easy answer and then stop thinking. Rather, obedience rejects the easy answers of the status quo and thus requires one to think more deeply. The rejection of compromise is not the easy way out. One may consider the most effective situation in which one would want to return his draft card, but it is wrong to decide whether to do it or not on the basis of what will happen to him if he does. The question rather is, What should I do? Having made that decision, the consequences are no longer decisive. It is not possible or desirable to ignore the context of one's action, but the context may not be the starting point nor one's authority.

To refuse to be expedient or accept compromise must mean a willingness to accept suffering and even death. The way of noncompromise is potentially tragic, for it blocks off the only road out of commitment, namely compromise. It means that decisions will not be made on the basis of avoiding suffering, but on the basis of what is right and necessary. This is what is meant by taking up the cross, going the way of the cross. Discipleship is always costly. It is something different from "American religion in general," where faith is considered to be a nice feeling and religion becomes a justification for what we want to do. Rather, discipleship means to go the way of the cross. Bonhoeffer wrote that "when Christ calls a man, he bids him come and die."[13] It is something of what Che Guevara meant when he stated,

---

[13] Dietrich Bonhoeffer, *The Cost of Discipleship* (New York: Macmillan, 1949), p. 79.

"In revolution one either wins or dies." It means total commitment. It rules out compromise.

The issue of compromise finally comes down to whether one has a long- or short-range vision. If immediate consequences are most important, then they must be the judge. The radical, however, is one who would rather fail in a cause that will someday win than win in a cause that will ultimately fail. He does not choose his path because he is convinced that it will fail, but because he is convinced that ultimately it will be victorious. The Christian accepts the way of the cross, the way of suffering love, because he is persuaded that ultimately this way is more powerful and more redemptive than that of force and might. This is the message of the resurrection. The radical rejects compromise not because he wishes to be foolish but because he has a commitment to that which he believes will someday overcome. Although his action may appear to others to be foolish, it does not seem foolish to him. Thus he can say that he does not base his action on what the consequence of this action will be, but on whether or not that action corresponds with his vision of ultimate reality.

The reason the radical refuses to compromise on the basis of present circumstances is because he is guided by a vision of a new reality. He dreams of the kingdom of God, of swords being beaten into plowshares, of peace and justice. His hope is based not on *what is*, but *what could be*. This vision dare not be compromised, for to be disobedient means to lose hope; it means to fall into despair, weariness, and resignation. But to be obedient is to live in hope.

It has often been argued that those who refuse to compromise condemn themselves to irrelevancy by removing themselves from the conflict. These people say that to be "responsible" one cannot remain pure. But this can be turned around. Has the compromiser been bringing about basic social changes or have his compromises with the old order actually meant support for the status quo? Often his compromising makes acceptable what should never be accepted. Could it be that ultimately the noncompromising witness has the greater impact? The radical believes that faithful witness through the ages (e.g., the martyrs) has had more social impact than those who have attempted to conform to the present age. The radical does not say, "Because I am a sinner I must compromise," but rather, "Because I compromise, I am a sinner." The radical believes that those who wait to do good until everyone else starts to do good will be the last evil people on earth. Compromise and contextual ethics are too conservative, for they take the status quo too seriously.

When one takes a noncompromising stand, how can the trap of pride and self-righteousness be avoided? How can the radical be spared from the escapist mentality of other-worldliness, aloofness, and separatism? How shall he keep moral purity from insulating him from the needs of the world? These are concerns the radical must take seriously.

The answer is that the issue is not personal purity. This should not be the motivation for refusing to compromise. Personal purity cannot be achieved, neither in our own personal attitudes nor in our actions. To be related to society in any way is to participate in its sin. To pay taxes is to kill people in Vietnam. Private virtuousness is an attempt to escape from reality and responsibility. The issue is not personal moral purity, but rather the clarity of the witness. The reason for rejecting compromise is to avoid blunting and weakening the witness. The reason the witness against the war should not be compromised is that this witness is so desperately needed. To moderate the witness is to weaken it. The more straightforward the witness, the more impact it can be expected to have. One's focus must be the clarity of the witness.

The radical rejects compromise because of a profound concern about the ends that are hoped to be achieved. If the means and ends cannot be separated, then to compromise the means is in effect to compromise the ends. This does not mean that we refuse to accept partial goals. It does mean that we will not give up ultimate goals in order to achieve partial goals. Thus compromise is not seen as a sacrifice of private purity, but as a sacrifice of the goal, and ultimately support for the old order. The question then is not what is forbidden, but what is my witness. The Christian should not be trying to justify himself, but to witness and *be*.

Again it must be said that the form of the witness must be flexible. It is permissible to examine the form of the witness. The use of language or type of action must be related to the context of the witness. The content of the witness, however, should never be compromised. Again, the clarity of the witness is the issue. Instead of going the way of compromise, the radical Christian will live in obedience to Christ and witness to the new reality that is in our midst. The radical Christian will not compromise that vision for the "realism" of the old order.

CHAPTER FIVE

A Theology for Revolution

> I love my city, but I shall not stop
> preaching that which I believe is true;
> you may kill me, but I shall follow
> God rather than you.
>
> Socrates

Introduction

To be a Christian is to be a subversive, or at least that is
how he will be viewed by society. Since his loyalty is to one
who is beyond history, he cannot give his ultimate allegiance
to any government, business, class, or any other institution.
His views cannot be expected to coincide with the majority
view around him. He can be expected to be in continual conflict with the structures of the society, for to be at peace with
God means to be in conflict with the world. When a Christian is faithful to Christ and refuses compromise with the
demands of society, it is almost inevitable that he will be
looked upon by the power structures of that society as being
disloyal and subversive, and so he is. He is a person who
dares to call the whole society into question. He is a revolutionary.

We live in an era of revolution. It is almost a cliché to
talk about the rising expectations of oppressed people, move-

ments for social justice and guerilla warfare. Yet they are very real. Revolution is the dominant fact of our times. The war in Vietnam is a symbol for what is happening everywhere in the world. Enslaved peoples are preparing to throw off their chains. The class struggle is taking on new reality. The confrontation of black and white has only begun in the United States, and may well end in nightmarish violence and oppression. The present order may well be facing destruction.

Significantly, this movement toward liberation not only involves the lower classes, but reaches deeply into the middle and upper classes. The alienation and revolt of a large portion of youth from establishment values show how broad the liberation movement is. This search for new freedom is to be found in affluent America and Western Europe, throughout the Third World, and also in the socialist countries. As disenchantment with present social structures becomes more pervasive, the questions of revolution take on new urgency. They cannot be avoided.

We have maintained in this study that in spite of the conservative image commonly associated with Christianity, biblical faith includes a revolutionary vision. Even though Christianity has been branded by white colonialism, the atomic massacre of two hundred thousand Japanese civilians in Hiroshima and Nagasaki, racial bigotry, and the slaughter of Vietnamese by "Christian" U.S. firepower, the seeds of liberation and revolution are inherent in the biblical message. Note how many revolutionaries have been fostered unintentionally by Christian missions. We have made the case for the Christian being a revolutionary. Now we must examine how the radical Christian can relate to the revolution and deal more directly with the issues of revolution and social change.

The Nature of Revolution

Although we have been referring to revolution throughout this study, we must now be more specific in our definition of this term. Revolution is an astronomical term that can be understood in two ways. It can mean a complete circle, which ends where it started from. Thus a revolution would mean one group seizing power from another group and simply reversing the roles of oppressor and oppressed. This has been the meaning of most historical events that have been called revolutions and could be best illustrated by the term *coup d'etat*. One group takes power and basic conditions remain the same.

A more profound understanding of revolution is in the astronomical implication of going back to a preordained order, of restoring something that has been lost. Revolution at its best is thought of as restoration. The Anabaptists were revolutionary in their attempt to restore the ideals of the primitive church. The New Left is revolutionary in its attempt to recover a lost heritage of freedom and justice. The revolutionary rejects present conditions, for he believes that these conditions need not continue, that poverty and injustice are not inherent in human relationships.

Revolution as used here does not mean rapid social change, but fundamental social change. It refers to the radical nature of change rather than the speed of change, for rapid social change can also be counterrevolutionary. The important thing about the revolutionary is that he seeks radical change. The true revolutionary attacks the very basis of a civilization. The revolutionary aspect of the lunch-counter sit-ins in the South was that they were able to shake the whole Southern way of life. They struck at the very heart of the problem. With this definition we must call the American Revolution a war of independence, since its aim was not to alter radically the structure of the economy, slavery, or society in general, even though many of the early fathers were radicals. The revolutionary considers it more important to change the structure of society than to alter only the political structure. True revolution is more than the realization of the implicit ends of the old order. It must be radically different. Revolution points to the new. It means a radical departure from the old.

This definition of revolution is different from Camus' distinction between rebellion and revolution.[1] For Camus, rebellion has positive connotations while revolution has the negative connotation of absolutizing rebellion. Although he makes a valid point, revolution as used in this study excludes the absolutizing of rebellion, which would be considered to be counterrevolutionary as used here. Rebellion then can be either positive or negative. Revolution points to the restoration of a fallen order, to a new day of peace and justice.

Revolution is an attempt to close the gap between the ideal and the real. It is a struggle to move from the *is* to the *ought*. It is motivated by both a revulsion at the injustice of the present and a feeling of loyalty to something higher. Thus it is an attempt to move beyond the present to a future that seems within reach. Camus develops this theme.

> In every act of rebellion, the rebel simultaneously experiences a feeling of revulsion at the infringement of his rights and a complete and spontaneous loyalty to certain aspects of himself. Thus he implicitly brings into play a standard of values so far from being gratuitous that he is prepared to support them no matter what the risks.[2]

It means one is committed to a new course. As Camus put it, "Rebellion cannot exist without the feeling that, somewhere and somehow, one is right."[3] The revolutionary is a reformer. Che Guevara also had this vision of the guerilla.

> We must come to the inevitable conclusion that the guerrilla fighter is a social reformer, that he takes up arms responding to the angry protest of the people against their oppressors, and that he fights in order to change the social system that keeps all his unarmed brothers in ignominy and misery.[4]

The aim of revolution is freedom within a new order. Hannah Arendt notes that this is an important difference between

---

[1] Albert Camus, *The Rebel* (New York: Alfred A. Knopf, 1954), p. 106.

[2] *Ibid.*, pp. 13-14.

[3] *Ibid.*, p. 13.

[4] Che Guevara, *Guerrilla Warfare* (New York: Monthly Review Press, 1961), p. 17.

revolution and war. Only rarely, she claims, has freedom been the aim of war.[5]

The structures of society can be changed. From a brief study of history it becomes obvious that society can be radically transformed. Consider the change that came about through the Reformation, the rise of Puritanism, the Industrial Revolution, or the Civil Rights Movement. This, however, is not the issue. More important is to keep in mind that change does not necessarily mean progress or betterment. Before we work for change, therefore, we must be very clear what that change is which we wish to bring about. It is not difficult to work sincerely for change only to find the remedy to be worse than the sickness. The goal of change must be radical. The Black Power Movement is right in rejecting integration of Blacks into a decadent, middle-class, white society. A reactionary project is to work for more opportunities for Black people in the military machine. The tragedy of Africa today is that Black people are taking over the oppressive roles of the departing white rulers rather than developing revolutionary new ways of relation to each other. The Africans are proving to be just as oppressive as were their white masters. (Note the current civil war in Nigeria.) Change does not justify itself. It must lead to new kinds of relationships. Joffre Stewart, a Black anarchist, has stated this most forcefully.

> . . . It is a mistake to mobilize nonviolent pressures to obtain integration in the armed forces. Why be nonviolent in order to improve your opportunity for learning how to kill or to increase your opportunity for getting killed? That issue may be going out of date now that colored boys are fast getting equal chances with white boys to blast whole countries off the map with weapons that can poison the human race. But I insist that if we are serious about nonviolence we can have no interest in raising demands for integration into war jobs or security work. And I do hope that nonviolence is not being used to improve the condition of the Negro only in order to raise his morale that he may become a more avid Chink-killer, Commie-killer, Kike-killer or whoever

5 Hannah Arendt, *On Revolution* (New York: Viking Press, 1963), p. 2.

it is that may be indicated to us at the next turn of the diplomatic game.[6]

Changing society cannot be an end in itself, for the new can be worse than the old. One must keep in view the quality of human existence that will result from the change. Every new form must come under the same judgment as old forms.

Change is inevitable. It is something that must be lived with, for if the biblical understanding of reality is correct, change cannot be prevented. Revolution is not a new thing. Every ruling class in history that has insisted that its rule was destined to last forever has been shown to be wrong. The rule of an elite is never permitted to last very long. Every oppressor and tyrant will be overthrown. The Bible calls this the judgment of God. Reality is not static; therefore, we cannot preserve what is.

Since a static society is impossible, the conservative attempt to maintain the status quo is both naive and dangerous. The most dangerous approach of all to revolution is to try to stifle it. How is it possible to mummify an old society that is pregnant with the new? If reality is not static, then we can see that violence is the result of the frustration of change. Change is inevitable. The question is whether that change will come violently or nonviolently. But that question can be answered only by those in control. Change will come, and if it cannot come nonviolently, then it will come violently. The amount of violence involved in this process depends on the determination of the oppressors to hold on to their privileged position in the world. Basically, violence comes not from those seeking change, but from those preventing change.

It is a tragedy that the United States is at present the main counterrevolutionary force in the world. They are seeking to put down revolutions and prevent change both at home and around the world. The revolutions should not be squelched, for to defend the status quo or attempt to return to the past is the most destructive of all. At this time of

---

[6] Joffre Stewart, "Some Implications of Nonviolence in the Montgomery Resistance Movement" (Reprinted from *Balanced Living*, December, 1961).

social crisis when both conservatives and liberals are moving to a frenzied support of the establishment, the Christian should accept the collapse of the old and welcome the signs of a new order.

Not only is it wrong to try to stop a revolution; a revolution is actually needed. The liberal dream of reforming the old structures does not come to grips with the reality of the system that continues to oppress the people of the Third World, refuses to meet the needs of the poor at home, and suppresses creativity and sensitivity as it forces people into meaningless roles over which they have no control. The threat of a totally managed and controlled society, not unlike 1984, increases as our bourgeois-technocratic-bureaucratic system escalates the pressure for conformity and containment. Our system is leading not to the liberation of man, but to a new age of enslavement where central decision making and control reduce man to an object. The one sign of hope is the increasing rebellion against this system, a rebellion that cuts across class and age barriers.

The present system has proved itself incapable of solving our problems. Bureaucratic structures can be quite efficient in dealing with small problems, but seem to be totally incapable of solving the more pressing problems of our world. The most we can do in our cities is to hire more police to keep the lid on. Who is to solve these problems? The business community is so out of touch with the oppressed that it doesn't even understand the problem. Besides, its goal is incurably profit, not the humanization of society. Will governmental structures solve the problems? They show little indication of making the massive effort that would be necessary, and when they do make small efforts, they become tangled in bureaucratic red tape. The war on poverty is a classic example.

We reject the bourgeois liberal contention that all change must be rational, orderly, and within the limits of the present system. The liberal believes that the tendency for progress is incorporated into the very nature of our institutions. Thus he is forced to believe that continual progress is being made;

even while poverty, starvation, militarism, and racism are on the increase. This view is actually a total commitment to the present system and a refusal to understand how disorderly, irrational, and violent the present system is. Because of his support for the status quo, the liberal fails to develop alternatives to existing structures and thus is unable to create meaningful solutions to our problems. When a train is headed toward destruction there is little point in adjusting the controls. The need is to get the train headed in a different direction.

The New Left has at this point often been charged with anti-intellectualism and utopianism. These charges are unfair. Since the radical has rejected the assumptions and definitions of the system, he has few resources to rely on for analysis and reflection. He needs to strike out on uncharted paths and must rely heavily on experimentation, for he has found the old answers and definitions inadequate for the future. His rejection of the assumptions of the present system does not make him anti-intellectual. Is it more dangerous to consider the impossible as possible, or so to limit the possibilities that one cannot see beyond the present? The real utopianism is to believe that the present system can solve problems that it is in fact unable to cope with.

The radical understands that the institutions of our society were developed in another era under very different conditions and in response to different needs. Today these institutions are bankrupt and unable to deal with our situation. Note the stagnation and repressiveness of our educational institutions, for example. Institutions harden as they age, and as they try to preserve themselves they close themselves to the future. For institutions to survive they must be reproduced and continually reborn. What is needed is the development of new institutions to replace the old, just as the present institutions were developed in another era to replace the institutions of that era. We need revolution, not reform.

A Christian Theory of Social Change

The Christian response to our revolutionary age must be

to stand with the exploited. To be faithful to the biblical heritage and to be a responsible member of society will mean support for those who seek to escape from their bondage. The Christian should be identifying with the oppressed, rather than with the oppressor. He should be more concerned about the suffering of the poor than with the "dilemmas" of the President. It is worse than hypocritical to talk about "love and brotherhood" when what is really meant is the perpetuation of a system of organized exploitation and injustice. However, while the Christian should not be in the business of condemning the oppressed people who are overthrowing their chains of oppression, neither dare he wholeheartedly embrace everything in the revolutionary movements. The revolutionaries stand under the same qualification as do the oppressors. The obedient Christian points to the new reality regardless of situation or consequence. He will compromise that vision neither for oppressor nor for oppressed.

Our task then is to construct a Christian theory of social change. There are three basic approaches to social change. First there is the individualistic approach, of changing individuals. This is often identified with both political conservatism and religious fundamentalism. This theory maintains that the way to solve the race problem is to change the attitudes of all people on race, and then the social structures will take care of themselves. In effect this approach to social change ignores social structures. The second approach is to focus on the power structures. This is the approach of political liberalism, religious Puritanism, and the Communist Party. To solve the race problem, they would legislate new laws and outlaw discrimination. The communist approach, of course, would be the most radical attempt at changing the power structures. They are all the same, however, in that they see change as coming from the top down. Centralization of power is seen as a solution to most any social problem.

The third approach, which will occupy the remainder of this chapter, is a synthesis of Anabaptist and New Left strategy. This approach sees change as coming from the bottom up, through the establishing of new alternatives within community, and the inbreaking of a new order. This approach will seek to avoid the false debate between those who would work with structures and those who would work with individuals.

Radical change must come from the bottom up. The most positive hope within the New Left concept of revolution is the rejection of top-down reform and centralization of power. One of the tragedies of communist revolutions has been their reinforcement of the power of the state and greater centralization. With the increased threat to freedom that comes with centralization, it is significant to stress decentralization and participatory democracy. The picture of one who would subjugate the entire universe in order to establish new values is not a happy one. Its means and ends would necessarily be totalitarian. The point of the New Left is not to try to take over the power structures (the liberal dream which makes no sense anyway), but to question the presuppositions of the structures, to show that they are in fact irrelevant, and that they have no power.

Both guerilla movements and the movement in the United States have discovered that the power of large structures is deceiving. Giant monsters can be immobilized by committed groups or communities. The early church did not try to take over the Roman Empire or change it. They simply believed and acted as though it was not the center of history, and this attitude threatened the Romans to such an extent that they felt forced to stamp out the church. Likewise the Anabaptists shook the whole of Europe with their attempt to live a new kind of life.

There are at least three aspects to working at change from the bottom up. First comes a clear understanding and analysis of the system that controls us. Then we must begin the creation of a new self-identity. This involves getting rid of bourgeois values and the development of new life styles and relationships, both personal and societal. Third, we need to discover actions that will disrupt the old and help point to the new. The sit-ins during the Civil Rights Movement are one example of this. We need to begin to set in motion forces that the larger society will find impossible to ignore.

The argument is commonly raised that revolution must be rejected because it is dangerous to destroy structures that were built over a long period of time and still provide stability. This is a valid concern, which is answered by the New Left model for revolution. This approach does not advocate destroying the structures of society from the top, but from the bottom. In this approach new structures will be built to take the place of the old structures before they crumble, thus avoiding total chaos. The aim is to build new structures whose very existence will cause the old to crumble.

Although there is a centralization of power in our society, the problem must not be attacked from the center. The action should be on the periphery. The real center of power is with creative minorities who operate on the edge, on the cutting edge of society. They are closer to the real action than those who are in the power centers. The important changes in history have come not through people getting themselves in power, but through people who had the courage to break from the existing structures and begin to create new alternatives outside the system. We now call them pioneers. The radical will not work through the power structure in order to take it over. Neither will he wait until the establishment is ready to accept his ideas, for he may very well spend his whole life waiting as so many have done. He begins to act now on the vision. He is building a new society which will replace the old.

The radical approach is not only to suggest alternatives; it is to *be* and to live those alternatives. It is to live in the new reality. If we believe in the coming of the kingdom and the revolution, then the central issue must be how we are to relate to that new reality. The radical view is that although the kingdom is not yet complete, we live in the light of both what has come and what we expect to come. Even though the old political order is still very much here, we live as if it had passed away. We no longer support the structures of racism. We stop supporting oppressive structures such as the tobacco and liquor establishment, which has had such a degrading and murderous effect on so many people. We join the revolution by struggling against the evil and suffering of the present and by living now by the standards of the future. In this way the kingdom is made concrete. It makes little sense to fight for some value in the future. We must embody that value now. As Todd Gitlin has put it,

> If we believe in the possibility, however remote, of a new order of things, then the unfolding of a community movement must bear within it some seeds of that new order.[7]

The real division in Christian ethics between the radicals and the liberals concerns the method of relating to the kingdom. The liberal (and most fundamentalists, too!) will argue that although the kingdom is coming, we must live in the realities of the present order and make our decisions on that basis, rather than on the basis of the future order. That is why they reject noncompromise and pacifism. They wish to be realistic. The liberal hopes that through reforms he will gradually be able to bring in the kingdom. The Anabaptist has no such hopes. He knows that he will never be able to create the kingdom and neither can the liberal. He does not identify the "great society" or its successors with the kingdom. The Anabaptist simply tries to live in the light of the revolution that has already occurred and is coming. We are not called to make a sick world well. We are called to act well. That is a powerful political act in itself. It means being the revolution. Camus puts the same idea into somewhat different language.

> Rebellion, in fact, says — and will say more and more explicitly — that revolution must try to act, not in order to come into existence at some future date in the eyes of a world reduced to acquiescence, but in terms of the obscure existence that is already made manifest in the act of insurrection. . . . Instead of killing and dying in order to produce the being that we are not, we have to live and let live in order to create what we are.[8]

The answer to the question of how this approach is revolutionary comes from both liberals and conservatives. The

---

[7] Todd Gitlin, "The Battlefields and the War," *The New Student Left*, ed. Mitchell Cohen and Dennis Hale (Boston: Beacon Press, 1966), p. 133.

[8] *The Rebel*, p. 252.

answer given to the Anabaptists is that if we followed the Sermon on the Mount, if we took the teaching of Jesus literally, our society would collapse. They argue that "being responsible" means compromising the Christian ethic for the sake of national defense, economic stability, and political realism. They correctly understand the revolutionary implications of a radical Christian ethic! Thus to be obedient to Christ is to be revolutionary. One cannot be revolutionary and yet accept the basic essentials of our civilization. Communism is not revolutionary because it uses the same methods as capitalism: propaganda, uniformity, and manipulation. Power struggles are not revolutionary. Only living in the light of the kingdom is truly revolutionary.

It is instructive to note how Jesus approached the question of revolution and how similar his situation was to that of our own. Jesus had basically four options of relationship to society to choose from. (1) He could have become a Sadducee. The Sadducees were the conservatives of the time, having compromised and sold out to the Roman conquerors. They were the people with privilege and "influence" on the power structures. Jesus rejected trying to work through the power structures. (2) He could have joined the Pharisees, who separated their faith from life. They were uncompromising in matters of religion, but compromised with the Romans on "secular matters." For them, religion dealt only with the spiritual realm. (3) Jesus' third option was to escape to the desert and live a life of purity in an Essene community. Any association with society was considered a compromise with it. (4) The fourth and possibly most appealing option was to join the zealots, a guerilla force dedicated to overthrowing the Roman rule in Palestine. At least one, and probably more of Jesus' disciples were zealots. Jesus died as a revolutionary, for crucifixion was a political punishment. It is clear, however, that Jesus rejected the approach of the zealots. Instead he chose a fifth alternative: he called together a group of followers and began teaching a new way of life, pointing to the coming of the new era. Because of this, the

Romans killed him for being a revolutionary. This approach is here assumed to be the most revolutionary of all.

The Christian vision of the new reality includes not only a new society, but also new people. This also is no vague hope for the future, but can be a present reality. The revolutionary is one whose life has been changed. Guilt, despair, or hate are not motivation for the true revolutionary. To repudiate the old is not enough to liberate man for a new life style. His action must be based on a new reality that he has experienced. He must begin to live in a new reality which gives him strength and vision. If the only way really to confront the system is with one's life, then it is most important that radicals begin living lives that are revolutionary.

One problem of revolutions in the past has been that they separated liberation of whole social classes from liberation of the individual. If the social class is liberated from domination from the outside but continues to dominate its own people, liberation has in reality not taken place. We must talk of both personal and social salvation, for they cannot be separated.

The true revolutionary is one who knows who he is and why he is rebelling. Thus he does not easily fall into the trap of bitterness, unscrupulous ambition, or pleasure in seeing others destroyed. The one who is concerned about revenge for past wrongs is not revolutionary, for he is living in the past, not in light of the new that is coming. Camus writes that rebellion against evil is a search for unity.[9] But for the Christian, rebellion is based on a unity that has already been found. Sin is the opposite of radical. As Eagleton puts it,

> The vagrant and the sinner are the precise opposite of the *rebel*, who needs to be an authentic man to rebel, and establishes himself as such in the act of rebellion. To sin is to be a tramp, not a revolutionary.[10]

The radical acts not out of guilt, but for liberation. His

---

[9] *Ibid.*, p. 101.

[10] Terrence Eagleton, *The New Left Church* (Baltimore: Helicon Press, 1966), p. 164.

concern is not so much getting for others what he has, but getting rid of what he should not have. He must go beyond being able to identify the oppressor out there to realizing that I am also being oppressed, and that I must act not because I believe I should do something about that problem, but because I feel that oppression myself and must act for my own survival. We need a politics of liberation rather than a politics of guilt.

The revolutionary is one who is free, and to be free means to be defined by the new reality. When the slave defines himself as a child of God rather than a slave, he is already a rebel, for his slavery is not what gives him his identity. The slave who rebels simply denies that anyone is his master. He refuses to be defined in terms of a slave-master relationship, for he lives by a new reality. This is the message of the gospel: that man can be set free. The theologian Emil Brunner, describing the divine-human encounter, writes,

> . . . What happens is not something that short-circuits man as a free subject, that estranges him from himself, but something on the contrary that alone makes him really free and truly active. The reason for this is that it frees him from a life in contradiction to a life in the truth, and heals and integrates his will and makes it genuinely his own, a will which when sinful was never truly *his* will, but lay under the domination of an alien power. To be led by the Spirit of God is not to be possessed. On the contrary, it is to be liberated from possession, from the alien domination of evil.[11]

Rebellion is the refusal to be considered an object. It is to know that one has worth in spite of any historical phenomenon. The rebel is one who refuses to live in the box assigned to him. He has discovered freedom. Even chains or prison cannot enslave a free person.

Those who have changed the world have been those who have despised it. The revolutionary does not accept society as it is; in fact he equates it with injustice. He begins to say no to it and liberates himself from its control. The march on the Pentagon in 1967 was important in that tens of thousands

---

[11] Emil Brunner, *The Christian Doctrine of the Church, Faith, and the Consummation* (Philadelphia: Westminster Press, 1962), p. 13.

there proclaimed that that institution no longer had power over them.

The revolutionary is one who has accepted death. Even death no longer has any power over him. The Christian believes that death is not evil, that worse things can happen than death. The revolutionary does what needs to be done even though it may mean his own death. That for him is not as repulsive a thought as is surrender and compromise. He lives in hope that death is not the end, that even in spite of death there is yet hope.

The revolutionary is one who lives by a vision. He is not a nihilist. As Camus has affirmed, "The most elementary form of rebellion, paradoxically, expresses an aspiration to order."[12] This does not mean that one should fear the negative. A revulsion to evil is very much in order. The important thing is that one knows what he is for, so that he will be free to react to events around him.[13] But the important part of his message is what he affirms. He is not interested in denying authentic meanings and traditions from the past. He is looking to a new order. The central thrust is not tearing down the old but building the new community.

The life style described here implies a separation of the radical from the larger society. This is true not because the radical wishes to be separate, but because his witness of necessity sets him apart. When Senator Fulbright started criticizing the Vietnam war, he was no longer invited to the White House. This should not trouble the radical. Whoever criticizes a person for being too alienated from society should be suspected of being perhaps too well adjusted to society. There is nothing wrong with being maladjusted in a sick society. How can a moral man be respectable in an immoral society? It is in the name of respectable people that so much evil is perpetrated. The radical must not, however, become so separated from the world that he is no longer able to

---

[12] *The Rebel,* p. 23.

[13] It is significant that moderates will accuse a person of being negative when he points to any injustice. Those who seek respectability do not appreciate having the unrespectability of society exposed.

communicate with it. One must find ways to continue communication without compromising the witness.

We have been discussing the idea of changed people. Although change must begin with oneself this does not imply individualism. It is grounded in people in relationship, rather than alienation. To be authentic, one must be part of a community, for it is in relationship that man comes to know himself and is fulfilled. The radical is able not only to talk about man, but also to talk to man. In an alienated society, just to be a part of a community is a radical act. To share in intimacy with others is to live in wholeness. As Eagleton explains it,

> The radical response to an alienated society is the response of *community* — community as the way of life in which all men can be simultaneously free subjects, present to each other without mutual exploitation. The radical response, therefore, is to affirm that men can be free only in genuine equal relationship, not by avoiding relationship . . . or by enslaving others to insure one's own precarious freedom. . . .[14]

Community is the third alternative to the totalitarianism of collectivism and the alienation of individualism.

Community is a relationship in which the individual and collective are tied together. There is no community without unique, separate, and free individuals; otherwise it is a mass, or a tyranny of the group. But a true community is more than a group of individuals. They are bound together by a covenant that is deeper than what they bring to the group. From their separateness they feel a oneness. Community is where one can freely be for others. It is a prototype of the kingdom. In fact, it is the beginning of the kingdom in present reality.

To be a part of a community is especially important for people in the movement. They need a community in which they receive love, acceptance, and strength to continue, a group with which they can share deeply. Not only must this occur if one hopes for this kind of society, it is also important for perspective and support in one's radical activity. People

[14] Eagleton, p. 166.

must be involved in the movement for more than just the fulfillment of their own needs. They should be involved because their needs have already been fulfilled, because they are free to work and relate. It is very easy for a radical to be isolated and rendered ineffective or co-opted. A community of support will help him to remain stable in the face of instability. It will enable him to face the threat of suppression and suffering. This does not necessarily mean communal living or communities of love, but groups of people who have a common commitment and who meet regularly to share their hopes and fears, joys and frustrations. These fellowships will also serve as a basis for decision making. In a fragmented society, it is important for people to share with others their struggles with decisions. Decisions and analyses of strategies should be made collectively. Actions should not be taken in isolation from others in the movement.

Community must be also seen within the revolutionary strategy of building parallel structures. The movement and the church at its best should be a parabolic community, embodying those ideals it wishes to proclaim to the world. It is the beginning of the revolution. By its very existence the parabolic community, or parallel structure, makes its proclamation to the world. The parallel structure serves three basic functions. First it unmasks the moral bankruptcy and contradictions of the society around it. The free university exposes the impersonal university for what it is. It brings to light the hidden and focuses attention on the inconspicuous. Second, it points to a new reality. It indicates new possibilities. It points beyond what is to what could be. It means raising new alternatives, asking questions that are not being asked, and challenging commonly held assumptions. Third, it helps create new alternatives. The radical is the pioneer. He does what the conservative is afraid to do. So it is that the parallel structure is free to try new approaches, to do the unthinkable. Out of the experimentation with new forms, the radical community can show concretely to the larger society not only what can be done, but what in fact is already being done. In this way people can begin to feel in themselves and see in the society around them the difference between the old and the new.

A brief history of some of the revolutionary actions of the church may be helpful at this point. In spite of its often conservative stance, the church has had a revolutionary function in Western society. When the church is true to its message, it is not serving as the chaplain for society, the justifier of the status quo, or a cathartic outlet for frustration and rebellion. The church has had an important role in developing new structures. At the times when the church has shown vitality, it has been the community most free to find new models for living. The modern ideas of hospitals, schools and universities, mental care, public health, and training for the blind have come out of the church. Hospitals began not because Christians petitioned the government for new structures, but because they had concern for sick people and began caring for them. This was a revolutionary idea, and eventually the government took up the task. The seeds for the ultimate elimination of slavery in the Roman Empire were sown by the early Christians making no distinction between slave and free. It can be argued that the Quakers and Methodists did more to change society and influence Anglo-Saxon democratic traditions than did Anglican and Puritan politicking. Today, the radical community needs to take the dominant problems of our society and find new creative ways of relating to them. Those who are obedient to Christ are the ones who have a view of the eschaton, and who begin living it and making it present now. Ultimately they believe that real power is not in bureaucratic institutions, but in liberated communities living by the new reality.

The aim of revolution is freedom. But if the result of a revolution is continued slavery and oppression, then the revolution has been betrayed. The revolutionary must strive for more than the breaking of the bonds of slavery; he must also live for freedom. What a parody it is that although in the last two centuries man overthrew the chains of monarchy and religion, he was barely free before he had created new and even more intolerable fetters. The goal of freedom cannot be used to justify any means, for too often freedom has been used to justify what could not be supported on rational grounds. We must clearly reject the current term "by any means necessary." This unqualified principle means that even stalinization or fascism may be "necessary." The radical must be careful not to accept absolute freedom, for any principle made into an absolute is dangerous. Absolute freedom cuts one off from the roots of his own existence, from the values he would pursue, and from his brother. The liberation of man as an absolute ends in the terror of the French Revolution. Absolute freedom ends in murder and finally suicide.

Participatory democracy must be seen as both a means and an end. It is not a luxury; it is a necessity. If freedom is not at the very core of the pursuit of freedom, it will be lost in the struggle. The rebel must be careful not to destroy his solidarity with the rest of humanity. An individualistic view of freedom is a contradiction in terms, for it denies responsibility and the freedom of the other. The radical should recognize that the source of his existence (God) is that which binds him to his neighbor. To cut off the neighbor then is to strike at one's own existence. If the radical is to keep free of a totalitarian mentality, he must never deny the freedom of the other. Camus makes the same point.

> The rebel undoubtedly demands a certain degree of freedom for himself; but in no case, if he is consistent, does he demand the right to destroy the existence and the freedom of others. He humiliates no one. The freedom he claims, he claims for all; the freedom he refuses, he forbids everyone to enjoy. He is not only the slave against the master, but also man against the world of master and slave. Therefore, thanks to rebellion, there is something more in history than the relation between mastery and servitude. Unlimited power is not the only law.[15]

People should never be reduced to objects or means, for to do so is to deny one's own humanity. The theology of the computer is wrong, for it presupposes that people should be controlled and reduced to facts. Any manipulation of persons must be resisted by the radical. The attempt must always

---

[15] *The Rebel,* p. 284.

be made to make the vision of participatory democracy concrete.

We have argued that change must come from the bottom up and through the creation of new alternatives. Our last point in outlining a theory of social change is that the revolution is not something we create, but is the inbreaking of a new order. It is similar to the way the Renaissance replaced the Middle Ages. That was not consciously planned and produced. People just began living differently, for a new era had come. The kingdom of God is not an ethical society that we gradually develop through our acts of love and service. Rather, it is a new reality breaking into history. It is not what we create. This eschatological perspective is understood both by Marxists and Christians. Herbert Aptheker, the American Marxist theoretician, asks, "Would it not appear that there must be some irresistible force working within all hitherto existing social systems which, despite the apparent omnipotence of the rulers, succeeds in terminating their rule and basically altering those systems?"[16] This view is difficult for rationalists to accept, yet is an important aspect of radicalism. The power of the prophets has been their ability to proclaim the coming of a new era. Is it not true that change comes as a surprise, that events never quite happen as expected? It means the rejection of the totalitarian claim that man is the master of his own destiny. It is an affirmation of openness to the future.

Christian theology describes this inbreaking as *kairos*, a Greek word for time. In distinction from *chronos* (linear time), *kairos* is a time pregnant with new possibilities, a turning point in history. It refers to those decisive times when the future breaks into the present, when the eternal breaks into the temporal and transforms it. For the Christian, one such event was the coming of Jesus as the Christ. To be conscious of the *kairos* is to be grasped by the urgency and destiny of the times. It is the expectation of a new time in history. Paul Tillich saw Marxism as being the movement most con-

---

[16] Herbert Aptheker, *On the Nature of Revolution: The Marxist Theory of Social Change* (New York: New Century Publishers, 1959), p. 5.

scious of an anticipation of the *kairos*. *Kairos* implies anticipation. In discussing socialism Tillich wrote,

> It is through anticipation that the proletariat experiences the
> meaning of its existence. It is through anticipation that the inner
> contradiction of our epoch becomes evident, just as the antici-
> pation of the early Christians made them aware of the demonic
> powers which ruled their world. When the proletariat awoke from
> its stupor under early capitalism and became conscious of itself
> as proletariat, a new anticipation was thereby brought to birth.
> Indeed, the one did not happen without the other. The anticipa-
> tion of the proletariat, in the religious sense of the word, ex-
> presses both the non-possession of what is anticipated, the living
> in the proletarian situation, and the anticipatory possession of
> what is hoped for, the creative tension in which the present is
> potentially overcome. Just because of his anticipation the prole-
> tarian is no longer *only* a proletarian.[17]

Quakers use the term "Lamb's War" to describe God's
action in bringing in the kingdom and our participation in
the struggle against evil. This concept comes from the book
of Revelation and points to the truth that God is the one
who will overcome evil. It implies that we are to fight not
with the weapons of the old order, but rather by living in
the kingdom and using the weapons of the Spirit. The Lamb's
War is God's revolution.

To assert that we cannot bring in the kingdom through
our own effort does not mean inactivity or resignation. Rather
we accept the kingdom as a gift, as a given, and begin living
in it. We participate in movements for social justice, because
we already live by that new vision. We participate in demonstrations to witness to what God has already done and
what he will do. To say that we will not bring in the new
era does not deny the possibility that it may be created
through our actions. The point is that we do not create it.
It is bigger than we are.

This attitude is important for several reasons. It is a safe-
guard against becoming a victim of one's own sense of
urgency. Desperate action is usually not radical action, for
despair is not the basis for revolution. Nothing is more evil

---

17 Paul Tillich, *The Protestant Era* (Chicago: University of Chicago
Press, 1948), pp. 171-172.

than the attempt to create the kingdom no matter what the cost or by what means. This is the crusade, the inquisition, the worst of religious fanaticism. It is important for the revolutionary to realize that time is on his side. Therefore he can endure defeat without despair.

This attitude is important also inasmuch as the notion that we can bring in the kingdom is the basis for totalitarianism. With the thought that we can bring in the kingdom comes the absolutizing of one's actions. They can no longer be qualified. Our task is not to force society to be good, but to confront it with its evil and show it a vision of the good. We should not seek to order society (creating order answers the wrong question anyway), but should point to the new.

The goal of the revolution is not to seek power over others. The radical does seek power over his own life, but does not wish to control others. He understands that things would not be better if he had the power, but that power is the problem. The problem is that the powerful rule over the weak and call themselves benefactors. To begin to manipulate and control others is to develop another oppressive system. The revolutionary rejects all servile relationships, including that to the revolution.

It is important to remain open to the future, for if one accepts a fixed notion of the end, one has already become rigid. This is the New Left critique of the Old Left. Any revolutionary movement that has become absolutist can be dated to the time when it became frozen. Its adherents absolutize a view that may have been authentic at one point in history and fail to remain open to the change of history. They live in a past future. Someone has said that "a conservative is someone who worships a dead radical." It is a tragedy when a revolution ends with the Daughters of the American Revolution (D.A.R.). Radicals need to avoid substituting one absolute for another, for in contrast to the conservative who absolutizes the past, the radical is in danger of absolutizing the present and future. The way to remain open to history is not to try to control it. Revolution is an adventure with new possibilities, not ultimate answers.

We need to accept the fact that ultimately we cannot control our own destinies. It is a fascist mentality which tries to control the future, which tries to force the future through political or military means. To do this of necessity rejects openness to criticism or other alternatives. It is the denial of democracy, for democracy presupposes an openness to many possibilities. The desire to control the future lies behind American actions in Vietnam. Both individuals and communities must resist the temptation to control the future. Whenever people try to secure their future, they mess it up. This is because when they grasp for security they are no longer open to the future. Participatory democracy means openness to change, not the attempt to control the future. It is the bureaucrats who try to program and control change. The radical remains open to the future.

Toward a Revolution of Nonviolence

Thus far a case has been built for revolution. There has been no rationale, however, for violence. The structure of the argument thus far would logically lead one to reject violence as a means to achieving our ends. We shall now consider some aspects of a nonviolent revolution. First we shall deal with the issue of civil disobedience, and then with pacifism in relation to revolution.

Civil disobedience is at its very heart an affirmation, an act of faith. To defy a law on the basis of conscience is to affirm a higher law. It is to acknowledge that obedience to God is more important than one's allegiance to any institution. It is to affirm that man should not be defined by the institutions to which he attaches himself. Thus the willingness to defy a law is a disavowal of the totalitarian claims of the state or any other institution. It is to affirm that the state by its existence does not automatically have authority over the person. Berdyaev maintains that the idea that the state has authority over the person is heathen in origin and fundamentally un-Christian, for he sees Christianity as unreconcilable with any earthly authority.[18] It is wrong to grant the state authority to allow freedom. Freedom is not for the state to grant. Freedom must be rooted in persons, not institutions. Thus freedom can best be preserved by limiting the power of the state. Since it seems to be in the nature of the state to reach beyond its limits and make itself absolute, civil disobedience is actually a service to the state in that it helps impede its self-destructive tendencies. Civil disobedience helps people to affirm who they are. It reminds them that they do not belong to their country, corporation, or class. They belong to God.

The Christian will often be looked upon as an anarchist, because of his failure to give very much respect to any human authority or institution. Although he is close to anarchism he is not an anarchist, for he has a profound respect for God's laws and his responsibility to his fellow man. He will respect any laws, such as traffic laws, that are seen as contributing to freedom and brotherhood among men. But when any law becomes oppressive, he will disobey it.

Civil disobedience is a witness against an evil itself, and also against the immorality of silence and passive cooperation with evil. To cooperate with evil is to condone it. It is to live beside a napalm factory and do nothing to shut it down. We must never tolerate what is radically evil. All too often tolerance serves the cause of oppression, for the tyrant goes on his way while others remain silent and still. We must refuse cooperation with evil and actively witness against it.

We must reject the bourgeois view of law and order, a view that is more concerned with order than with justice. This view either fails to comprehend the violence and disorder of the status quo, or is a dishonest attempt to rationalize injustice. This does not mean that the revolutionary should be disrespectful of order; it means that he cannot accept the present order. Only those who understand the chaos of the present and are actually working for change may honestly call for law and order. Within an immoral society, it is often

---

[18] Nicolas Berdyaev, *The Realm of Spirit and the Realm of Caesar* (New York: Harper and Brothers, 1952), pp. 72-76.

the defendant in the courtroom who represents law and order rather than the judge. Often the attempt to stop crime results in punishment.

The radical is not afraid to see a collision between the forces of good and evil. Since he believes in the victory of truth over falsehood, he is happy to see the issues brought into the open. Refusing to cooperate with evil is seen as one way to force people to deal with the issues they have been ignoring. Civil disobedience is an act that cannot be ignored in a society that demands conformity. Often humanization can occur only after the inhuman forces have come under attack. One should not be surprised that these forces will not surrender, but through the cross one knows that they in fact have already been defeated. This action fits with the New Testament view of the church as being on the offensive. Even "the gates of hell will not prevail against it" (Matt. 16:18).

When civil disobedience takes the form of a boycott or other pressure tactics, care must be taken not to deny the freedom of others. The other person should always be left with a choice. This does not weaken the action, however. In a rent strike, the freedom of the owner should not be denied. He is given the choice of selling the building, lowering the rent, or fixing the building. The one choice he no longer has is to dehumanize the tenants. If man is ultimately not defined by his institutions, then his institutions can be attacked without denying his personhood. In fact, this may be a way of affirming it.

Civil disobedience can be an important method of securing freedom for society. No law has any meaning unless there is almost unanimous respect for it. No law can be enforced if even a small percentage of the people refuse to obey it. This can be an effective way of stopping injustices. How should the draft be stopped? By petitioning congressmen? Hardly. By killing the draft board members? This would only harden the system. The system can be destroyed by no longer respecting it or cooperating with it. The draft will collapse if a relatively small number will refuse to cooperate with it in any way. The major accomplishments in history have not been won by going through "proper channels," but by people who were willing to put their bodies on the line, who were willing to go into the streets to demonstrate their noncooperation with the old way. In a society where people have little power or influence, they always have the power to disrupt the oppressive systems.

We now must look at the relation of pacifism to revolution. Does pacifism have relevance in our modern revolutionary world? The argument of this study has been that a third alternative must be found to acquiescence to injustice and violent revolution. We are not limited to the two choices of violence and capitulation to oppression. The argument will be made here that a revolution has much more chance of success if it remains nonviolent. This is not, however, to argue for gradualism or liberalism. It means to be even more radical. Our assumption is that violent revolution is occurring because nonviolent revolution is not occurring.

The basic problem with a violent revolution is not that it is too radical, but that it is not radical enough; not that it brings too much change, but too little. Replacing the violence of the oppressor with the violence of the oppressed may bring some change, but is far too inadequate a change. To continue in the old forms of violence is not revolutionary. Violence always tends to be reactionary, no matter what objectives it may be used for. First of all it looks on people as objects. When one begins to rely on violence, he comes more and more to depend on it (escalation). Often it becomes romanticized. Its use causes other means to appear more and more ineffective and irrelevant. It is reactionary because the user becomes deluded into thinking that he is accomplishing much more than he really is. Finally, violence is undemocratic. Since it uses unprogressive means, its end will include these elements. If McLuhan is right that the medium is the message, then the medium of violence is finally the message of violence. Paul Goodman made an important point when he stated,

In this very bad society, I am in favor only of the kind of actions

I would want people to take in a better society.... I think whatever we do now should be a model for what people are to do
in the future.[19]

The argument that the opponent is using violence cannot
be accepted, since the model for a revolution cannot be based
on the old order. There is nothing radical about doing the
same thing the opponent is doing. Few, however, would use
so crass an argument for violence. Yet in subtle ways this
logic does come to the fore. It is very easy to adopt what
one is actually fighting against. There is always the temptation to meet evil on its own terms, but to react to the opponent is to be controlled by him. The pacifist argument is
that violence has a disastrous effect upon those who use it.
To fight fascism with fascism is to become a fascist. Rather,
we must fight evil on our own ground and our own terms.
Thus if democracy is under attack, that calls us to be all
the more democratic. To become less so is to admit defeat
already. To accept the standards of the opponent is to be
defeated by him. Nonviolence is the real method of liberation. It liberates even when it fails. It realizes within its
means the ends that are sought.

The Anabaptist approach to pacifism has been nonresistance rather than nonviolent resistance. A word must be said
here in favor of the Anabaptist position. To resist is to focus
one's attention on the evil being opposed. To do this is to
lose sight of the reason for resistance. However, nonresistance
has the danger of quietism and escapism. The answer must
be witness. Rather than centering attention on the evil, one
needs to stand up boldly to evil on the basis of the new
reality, pointing not to the evil, but to the new reality that
will expose the old for what it is. Direct-action tactics should
be thought of in terms of witness.

Part of the radicalness of pacifism is to be found in its
hope for the conversion of the opponent. This does not mean
seeking peace with the oppressor, but rather his conversion.
It is a call for the slave to repudiate his master as master,

---

[19] Quoted by Lionel Abel, "Seven Heroes of the New Left," *New
York Times Magazine*, May 5, 1968, Section 6, p. 129.

but not as man. It seeks to eliminate oppression, but not the oppressor. The pacifist takes this stand because he believes people can change. The oppressor needs liberation just as much as does the exploited.

Christian pacifism must take the cross seriously. It sees the cross as God's way of dealing with evil. But through the resurrection the way of suffering, defeat, and humiliation was proven to be victorious. The Christian takes this approach because he believes that the way of Christ will triumph. It is belief in the victory of weakness over power, of foolishness over wisdom. This presupposes, of course, a high view of eschatology, a strong faith in the coming of the new era. It also assumes a willingness to accept suffering. It means taking unnecessary suffering upon oneself. It means to make oneself vulnerable. In reality, however, being authentic always makes one vulnerable, for it implies living without defenses. This kind of action is illustrated by the returning of draft cards, an act that makes one much more susceptible to suffering. Nonviolence means a willingness to accept the suffering upon oneself that would fall upon the oppressors if they should change their lives. The Christian pacifist is prepared to accept suffering and death (as is the violent revolutionary).

The radical pacifist in our day must come to terms with the violent revolutionary who reasons that a short, violent revolution is far less destructive than the perpetual violence of our present exploitation. This argument has much validity; but it must be rejected, for it assumes that the consequences can be predicted and that the means justify the ends. Having rejected this argument, however, the radical pacifist may not dismiss it. We dare not take the road of liberal pacifism and hope to keep our hands clean by dissociating ourselves from those using violence. This cannot be done, for by being a part of Western society we have already helped the oppressors and benefited from the exploiters. We must stand with the oppressed people who are struggling for freedom. We must agree that the violence of the oppressed is qualitatively different from that of the oppressor. Who are we to tell the Vietnamese people to lay down their arms in face of the American destruction of their homes? It is one thing to tell the oppressor to stop fighting, but something quite different to tell the oppressed to accept defeat. Who are we to tell those who are being executed to be nonviolent? We must be able to understand why the oppressed go the way of violence, but at the same time realize that violence is self-defeating. While we can support the aim of the revolutionary, we cannot support his violent means. We dare not forsake our vision of the new humanity. We must still witness to that reality.

We need to recognize that the violent people in our society are not those struggling for liberation, but rather the leaders of our government, business executives, and university presidents; those who use their power to suppress change and who devise new and more efficient methods of killing and controlling people. These are the ones who are most violent and the ones the pacifist should oppose. We must work to unmask the hypocrisy of men like Lyndon Johnson and Richard Nixon, who call for nonviolence among the oppressed while they themselves have been so ready to use massive violence to maintain oppression.

The radical pacifist must definitely oppose those who would romanticize violence. The crusade mentality is not new, nor has it ever been very fruitful. It is not true that if we have one more bloodbath, then there will be peace and justice. Practically every murder ever committed was done with the belief that the world would be better without the victim. But violence does not bring change. Even Marx recognized that the basis for social change is not violence, but the inherent contradictions of the old order.

The radical lives in hope. The revolutionary already tastes the revolution that is coming. As the prophet Zechariah put it, "Not by might, nor by power, but by my Spirit, says the Lord of hosts" (Zech. 4:6).

Bibliography

CHAPTER I

Abel, Lionel. "Seven Heroes of the New Left," *New York Times Magazine*, May 5, 1968, Section 6, p. 30.

Ali, Tariq, ed. *The New Revolutionaries: A Handbook of the International Radical Left*. New York: William Morrow, 1969.

Bay, Christian. "Political and Apolitical Students: Facts in Search of Theory," *Journal of Social Issues*, XXIII (July, 1967), pp. 76-91.

Blumenthal, Richard. "SDS: Protest is Not Enough," *The Nation*, CCIV (May 22, 1967), pp. 656-660.

Brown, Donald R. "Student Stress and the Institutional Environment," *Journal of Social Issues*, XXIII (July, 1967), pp. 92-107.

Cohen, Mitchell, and Dennis Hale, eds. *The New Student Left*. Boston: Beacon Press, 1966.

Cooper, David, ed. *To Free a Generation*. New York: Collier Books, 1968.

Davidson, Carl. *The Multiversity: Crucible of the New Working Class*. Chicago: Students for a Democratic Society, 1967. (pamphlet.)

Dowd, Douglas F. "America Fouls its Dream," *The Nation*, CCIV (Feb. 13, 1967), pp. 198-203.

Feldman, Paul. "LID and the Student Movement," *LID News Bulletin*, VI (Winter, 1966), pp. 5-8.

Flacks, Richard. "The Liberated Generation: An Exploration of the Roots of Student Protest," *Journal of Social Issues*, XXIII (July, 1967), pp. 52-75.

Freedman, Mervin B. "The Post-Industrial Generation: Roots of Student Discontent," *The Nation*, CC (June 14, 1965), pp. 639-643.

Goodman, Paul. *Growing Up Absurd*. New York: Vintage Books, 1956.

Halliwell, Steve. "Personal Liberation and Social Change," *New Politics News/2* [August, 1967], pp. 12-13.

Harrington, Michael. *Toward a Democratic Left*. Baltimore: Penguin Books, 1968.

Hayden, Tom. "The Politics of 'The Movement,'" *Dissent*, XIII (January-February, 1966), pp. 75-87.

143

Hayden, Tom. *Student Social Action*. Chicago: Students for a Democratic Society, 1966. (pamphlet.)

Howe, Irving. "Berkeley and Beyond," *New Republic*, CLII (May 1, 1965), pp. 14-17.

Howe, Irving. *New Styles in "Leftism."* Reprinted from *Dissent* (Summer, 1965). (pamphlet.)

Jacobs, Paul, and Saul Landau. *The New Radicals*. New York: Vintage Books, 1966.

Kempton, Murray. "The March on Washington," *New Republic*, CIL (September 14, 1963), pp. 19-20.

Keniston, Kenneth. "The Sources of Student Dissent," *Journal of Social Issues*, XXIII (July, 1967), pp. 108-137.

Kopkind, Andrew. "Anti-Vietnam Politics," *New Republic*, CLIV (June 4, 1966), pp. 15-18.

Kopkind, Andrew. "New Radicals in Dixie," *New Republic*, CLII (April 10, 1965), pp. 13-16.

Kopkind, Andrew. "Radicals on the March," *New Republic*, CLIII (December 11, 1965), pp. 15-19.

Lens, Sidney. "The New Left and the Old," *The Progressive*, XXX (June, 1966), pp. 19-24.

Lynd, Staughton. *The New Radicals and Participatory Democracy*. Reprinted from *Dissent* (Summer, 1965) by Students for a Democratic Society, Chicago. (pamphlet.)

Lynd, Staughton. "Radical Politics and Nonviolent Revolution." *Liberation*, XI (April, 1966), pp. 13-19.

Lynd, Staughton. "A Radical Speaks in Defense of S.N.C.C.," *New York Times Magazine*, September 10, 1967, Section 6, p. 50.

Mills, C. Wright. *The Power Elite*. New York: Oxford University Press, 1956.

Minnis, Jack. *The Care and Feeding of Power Structures*. Chicago: Students for a Democratic Society, 1966. (pamphlet.)

Moore, Peter C. *Youth in Crisis*. New York: Seabury Press, 1966.

New Left Notes, January 21, 1966–August 29, 1969.

Newfield, Jack. *A Prophetic Minority*. New York: Signet Books, 1966.

Newfield, Jack. "Revolt Without Dogma: The Student Left," *The Nation*, CC (May 10, 1965), pp. 491-495.

O'Connor, James. "New Left: Beyond the Burning Moral Thing," *The Nation*, CCIII (July 4, 1966), pp. 20-22.

Oglesby, Carl, and Richard Shaull. *Containment and Change*. New York: Macmillan, 1967.

Oglesby, Carl. "Democracy is Nothing if it is Not Dangerous," an undated reprint from *The Peacemaker*.

Oglesby, Carl. *Let Us Shape the Future*. Chicago: Students for a Democratic Society. Speech given at march on Washington, November 27, 1965. (pamphlet.)

Oppenheimer, Martin. *Alienation or Participation: The Sociology of Par-*

ticipatory Democracy. Chicago: Students for a Democratic Society, 1966. (pamphlet.)

The Port Huron Statement. Chicago: Students for a Democratic Society, 1962. (pamphlet.)

Potter, Paul. Untitled speech at the April 17, 1965 march on Washington. New York: Students for a Democratic Society, 1965. (pamphlet.)

Reade, Ben. "Prophet of the Powerless," *Renewal* (October-November, 1965), pp. 16-22.

"Report from the Editors: The SDS March on Washington," *Studies on the Left*, V (Spring, 1965), pp. 61-70.

Riessman, Frank. *A Comparison of Two Social Action Approaches: Saul Alinsky and the New Student Left*. 1965. (mimeograph.)

Sampson, Edward E. "Student Activism and the Decade of Protest," *Journal of Social Issues*, XXIII (July, 1967), pp. 1-33.

Spence, Larry D. "Berkeley: What it Demonstrates," *Studies on the Left*, V (Winter, 1965), pp. 63-68.

Thoughts of the Young Radicals. A New Republic Book, 1966.

Trent, James W., and Judith L. Craise. "Commitment and Conformity in the American College," *Journal of Social Issues*, XXIII (July, 1967), pp. 34-51.

Unger, Irwin. "The 'New Left' and American History," *American Historical Review*, LXXII (July, 1967), pp. 1237-1263.

Wasserman, Harvey. "Reform, Not Revolution," *The Progressive*, XXXI (August, 1967), pp. 27-28.

Zinn, Howard. "Emancipation from Dogma," *The Nation*, CCII (April 4, 1966), pp. 385-387.

Zinn, Howard. *SNCC: The New Abolitionists*. Boston: Beacon Press, 1964.

CHAPTER II

Bainton, Roland H. "The Left Wing of the Reformation," *Journal of Religion*, XXI (April, 1951), pp. 124-134.

Bainton, Roland H. *Studies on the Reformation*. Boston: Beacon Press, 1963.

Bauman, Clarence. "The Theology of the Two Kingdoms," *Mennonite Quarterly Review*, XXXVIII (January, 1964), pp. 37-49.

Bender, Harold S. "The Anabaptists and Religious Liberty in the 16th Century," *Mennonite Quarterly Review*, XXIX (April, 1955), pp. 83-100.

Bender, Harold S. "The Pacifism of the Sixteenth Century Anabaptists," *Church History*, XXIV (1955), pp. 119-131.

Bender, Harold S. "The Response of Our Anabaptist Fathers to the World's Challenge," *Mennonite Quarterly Review*, XXXVI (July, 1962), pp. 196-207.

Bender, Harold S. "Walking in the Resurrection: The Anabaptist Doctrine of Regeneration and Discipleship," *Mennonite Quarterly Review*, XXXV (April, 1961), pp. 96-110.

Bossert, Gustav, Jr. "Michael Sattler's Trial and Martyrdom in 1527," *Mennonite Quarterly Review*, XXV (July, 1951), pp. 201-218.

Estep, William R. *The Anabaptist Story*. Nashville: Broadman Press, 1963.

Fischer, Hans. "Lutheranism and the Vindication of the Anabaptist Way," *Mennonite Quarterly Review*, XXVIII (January, 1954), pp. 27-38.

Friedmann, Robert. "Claus Felbinger's Confession of 1560," *Mennonite Quarterly Review*, XXIX (April, 1955), pp. 141-161.

Friedmann, Robert. "The Essence of Anabaptist Faith. An Essay in Interpretation," *Mennonite Quarterly Review*, XLI (January, 1967), pp. 5-24.

Friedmann, Robert. "Some Further Studies Pertaining to the Handbüchlein of 1558," *Mennonite Quarterly Review*, XXIX (July, 1955), pp. 223-231.

Gardner, Richard. "Brethren and Pacifism," *Brethren Life and Thought*, VIII (Autumn, 1963), pp. 17-37.

Geiser, Samuel. "An Ancient Anabaptist Witness for Nonresistance," *Mennonite Quarterly Review*, XXV (January, 1951), pp. 66-69.

Heimann, Franz. "The Hutterite Doctrines of Church and Common Life, A Study of Peter Ridemann's Confession of Faith of 1540, II," *Mennonite Quarterly Review*, XXVI (April, 1952), pp. 142-160.

Hershberger, Guy H., ed. *The Recovery of the Anabaptist Vision*. Scottdale, Pa.: Herald Press, 1957.

Hillerbrand, Hans J. "The Anabaptist View of the State," *Mennonite Quarterly Review*, XXXII (April, 1958), pp. 83-110.

Hillerbrand, Hans J. "An Early Anabaptist Treatise on the Christian and the State," *Mennonite Quarterly Review*, XXXII (January, 1958), pp. 28-47.

Hillerbrand, Hans J. *Die politische Ethik des oberdeutschen Täufertums*. Leiden: E. J. Brill, 1960.

Hillerbrand, Hans J. *The Reformation*. New York: Harper and Row, 1964.

Horsch, John. "The Struggle Between Zwingli and the Swiss Brethren in Zurich," *Mennonite Quarterly Review*, VII (July, 1933), pp. 142-161.

Jones, Rufus M. *Studies in Mystical Religion*. London: Macmillan, 1936.

Kiwiet, Jan J. *Pilgram Marbeck*. Kassel: J. G. Oncken Verlag, 1957.

Klassen, Peter James. "The Economics of Anabaptism, 1525-1560," *Mennonite Quarterly Review*, XXXVII (April, 1963), pp. 131-132.

Kreider, Robert. "Anabaptism and Humanism: An Inquiry into the Relationship of Humanism to the Evangelical Anabaptists," *Mennonite Quarterly Review*, XXVI (April, 1952), pp. 123-141.

Kreider, Robert. "The Anabaptist Conception of the Church in the

Russian Mennonite Environment, 1789-1870," *Mennonite Quarterly Review*, XXV (January, 1951), pp. 17-33.

Kreider, Robert. "The Anabaptists and the Civil Authorities of Strasbourg, 1525-1555," *Church History*, XXIV (1955), pp. 99-118.

Littell, Franklin H. "The Basis for Religious Liberty in Christian Belief," *Journal of Church and State*, VI (1964), pp. 132-146.

Littell, Franklin H. *The Free Church*. Boston: Starr King Press, 1957.

Littell, Franklin H. *The Origins of Sectarian Protestantism*. New York: Macmillan, 1952.

Lynd, Staughton. "Bicameralism from Below," *Liberation*, XII (July, 1967), pp. 15-19.

Novak, M. "The Free Churches and the Roman Church," *Journal of Ecumenical Studies*, II (1955), pp. 426-447.

Peachey, Paul. "Social Background and Social Philosophy of the Swiss Anabaptists, 1525-40," *Mennonite Quarterly Review*, XXVIII (April, 1954), pp. 102-127.

Peachey, Paul. *Die Sociale Herkunft der Schweizer Täufer in der Reformationszeit*. Karlsruhe: Verlag Heinrich Schneider, 1954.

Sommer, Donald. "Peter Ridemann and Menno Simons on Economics," *Mennonite Quarterly Review*, XXVIII (July, 1954), pp. 205-223.

Waltner, Erland. "The Anabaptist Conception of the Church," *Mennonite Quarterly Review*, XXV (January, 1951), pp. 5-16.

Wenger, John C. "The Schleitheim Confession of Faith," *Mennonite Quarterly Review*, XIX (October, 1945), pp. 243-253.

Williams, George H. *The Radical Reformation*. Philadelphia: Westminster Press, 1962.

Williams, George H. *Spiritual and Anabaptist Writers*. Vol. XXV: *Library of Christian Classics*. Philadelphia: Westminster Press, 1957.

Wiswedel, Wilhelm. "The Handbüchlein of 1558," *Mennonite Quarterly Review*, XXIX (July, 1955), pp. 212-223.

Yoder, John Howard. *The Christian Witness to the State*. Newton, Kansas: Faith and Life Press, 1964.

Yoder, John Howard. *Peace Without Eschatology?* Scottdale, Pa.: Mennonite Publishing House, 1954. (pamphlet.)

Zschäbitz, Gerhard. *Zur Mitteldeutschen Wiedertäuferbewegung nach dem Grossen Bauernkrieg*. Berlin: Rütten und Loening, 1958.

CHAPTERS III, IV, V

Ahmad, Eqbal. *Revolutionary Warfare*. Chicago: Students for a Democratic Society, [1967]. (pamphlet.)

Aptheker, Herbert. *On the Nature of Revolution: The Marxist Theory of Social Change*. New York: New Century Publishers, 1959. (pamphlet.)

Aptheker, Herbert. *The Nature of Democracy, Freedom, and Revolution*. New York: International, 1967.

Arendt, Hannah. *On Revolution*. New York: Viking Press, 1963.

Arendt, Hannah. "Reflections on Violence," *New York Review of Books*, XII, No. 4 (February 27, 1969), pp. 19-31.

Barnet, Richard J. *Intervention and Revolution: The United States in the Third World*. New York: World Publishing Company, 1968.

Berdyaev, Nicolas. *The Realm of Spirit and the Realm of Caesar*. Tr. Donald A. Lowrie. New York: Harper and Brothers, 1952.

Bonhoeffer, Dietrich. *The Communion of Saints*. Tr. R. Gregor Smith. New York: Harper and Row, 1960.

Bonhoeffer, Dietrich. *The Cost of Discipleship*. Tr. R. H. Fuller. New York: Macmillan, 1959.

Bonhoeffer, Dietrich. *Ethics*. Tr. Neville Smith. New York: Macmillan, 1955.

Breitman, George. *How a Minority Can Change Society*. New York: Merit, 1966. (pamphlet.)

Brinton, Crane. *The Anatomy of Revolution*. New York: Prentice-Hall, 1952.

Brown, Dale W. "The New Theological Radical," *Christian Century*, LXXXV (November 13, 1968), pp. 1431-1434.

Brown, Kenneth L. "Updating Brethren Values," *Brethren Life and Thought*, XII (Summer, 1967), pp. 18-23.

Brunner, Emil. *The Christian Doctrine of the Church, Faith, and the Consummation*. Tr. David Cairns. Philadelphia: Westminster Press, 1962.

Camus, Albert. *The Rebel*. Tr. Anthony Bower. New York: Alfred A. Knopf, 1954.

Castro, Emilio. "Conversion and Social Transformation," *Christian Social Ethics in a Changing World*, ed. John C. Bennett. New York: Association Press, 1966.

Cleaver, Eldridge. *Soul on Ice*. New York: Dell, 1968.

Cox, Harvey G. *On Not Leaving It to the Snake*. New York: Macmillan, 1967.

Cox, Harvey. *God's Revolution and Man's Responsibility*. Valley Forge, Pa.: Judson Press, 1965.

Cox, Harvey. *The Secular City*. New York: Macmillan, 1965.

Cullmann, Oscar. *Christ and Time*. Tr. Floyd V. Filson. Revised edition. Philadelphia: Westminster Press, 1964.

Cullmann, Oscar. *The State in the New Testament*. New York: Scribner, 1956.

Cunningham, Adrian, and Terry Eagleton. *'Slant Manifesto' Catholics and the Left*. London: Sheed and Ward, 1966.

Davies, James C. "Toward a Theory of Revolution," *American Sociological Review*, XXVII (February, 1962), pp. 5-19.

Debray, Regis. *Revolution in the Revolution?* Tr. Bobbye Ortiz. New York: Grove Press, 1967.

Dellinger, Dave. *The New Nonviolence*. Nashville: Southern Student Organizing Committee, [1966]. (mimeograph.)

Deming, Barbara. "On Revolution and Equilibrium," *Liberation*, XII (February, 1968), pp. 10-21.

Dewey, John. "Means and Ends," *Partisan Review*, XXXI (Summer, 1964), pp. 400-404.

Eagleton, Terrence. *The New Left Church*. Baltimore: Helicon Press, 1966.

Eddy, Sherwood. *Revolutionary Christianity*. Chicago: Willett, Clark, 1939.

Eichrodt, Walther. *Theology of the Old Testament*, Vol. I. Tr. J. A. Baker. Philadelphia: Westminster Press, 1961.

Eller, Vernard. "Protestant Radicalism," *Christian Century*, LXXXIV (November 1, 1967), pp. 1391-1395.

Eller, Vernard, "A Theology of Nonresistance," *Christian Century*, LXXXIII (December 14, 1966), pp. 1534-1537.

Ellul, Jacques. *The Presence of the Kingdom*. Tr. Olive Wyon. New York: Seabury Press, 1967.

Fanon, Frantz. *The Wretched of the Earth*. Tr. Constance Farrington. New York: Grove Press, 1963.

Faw, William R. "Christian Youth in Rebellion, Resistance, and Revolution," *Signs of the Time*. Elgin, Ill.: Church of the Brethren General Offices, 1967.

Finn, James. *Protest: Pacifism and Politics*. New York: Vintage Books, 1968.

Fischer, Louis. *Gandhi and Stalin*. New York: Harper, 1947.

Free [Abbie Hoffman]. *Revolution for the Hell of it*. New York: Dial Press, 1968.

Furfey, Paul Hanly. *The Respectable Murderers: Social Evil and Christian Conscience*. New York: Herder and Herder, 1966.

Goodman, Paul. *People or Personnel* and *Like a Conquered Province*. New York: Vintage Books, 1963.

Guevara, Che. *Guerrilla Warfare*. Tr. J. P. Morray. New York: Monthly Review Press, 1961.

Hanson, John R. "Ernst Troeltsch's Concept of Compromise," *Lutheran Quarterly*, XVIII (November, 1966), pp. 351-361.

Hentoff, Nat, ed. *The Essays of A. J. Muste*. New York: Bobbs-Merrill, 1967.

Hoekendijk, J. C. *The Church Inside Out*. Tr. Isaac Rottenberg. Philadelphia: Westminster Press, 1966.

Holy Bible.

Hordern, William. *Christianity, Communism, and History*. Nashville: Abingdon Press, 1954.

Johnson, Chalmers. *Revolution and the Social System*. Stanford, Cal.: The Hoover Institution on War, Revolution, and Peace, 1964.

Kennan, George F. "Foreign Policy and Christian Conscience," *The Atlantic*, CCIII (May, 1959), pp. 44-49.

Leiden, Carl, and Karl M. Schmitt. *The Politics of Violence: Revolution in the Modern World.* Englewood Cliffs, N.J.: Prentice-Hall, 1968.

Lens, Sidney. *Revolution and Cold War.* Philadelphia: American Friends Service Committee, 1962. (pamphlet.)

Liberation. 1960-1969.

Long, Edward LeRoy, Jr. *Conscience and Compromise.* Philadelphia: Westminster Press, 1954.

Lynd, Staughton, ed. *Nonviolence in America: A Documentary History.* New York: Bobbs-Merrill, 1966.

Macgregor, G. H. C. *The New Testament Basis of Pacifism.* New York: Fellowship of Reconciliation, 1936.

Macgregor, G. H. C. *The Relevance of the Impossible: A Reply to Reinhold Niebuhr.* London: The Fellowship of Reconciliation, 1941.

Malcolm X. *The Autobiography of Malcolm X.* New York: Grove Press, 1964.

Marcuse, Herbert. *An Essay on Liberation.* Boston: Beacon Press, 1969.

Marcuse, Herbert. *One Dimensional Man.* Boston: Beacon Press, 1964.

Marcuse, Herbert. "Repressive Tolerance," in R. P. Wolff, *et al.,* *A Critique of Pure Tolerance.* Boston: Beacon Press, 1965.

Marty, Martin E., and Dean G. Peerman. *New Theology No. 6.* New York: Macmillan, 1969.

Marx, Karl, and Friedrich Engels. *Basic Writings on Politics and Philosophy.* Ed. Lewis S. Feuer. Garden City, N.Y.: Anchor Books, 1959.

Mayer, Peter, ed. *The Pacifist Conscience.* Chicago: Regnery, 1967.

Memmi, Albert. *The Colonizer and the Colonized.* Boston: Beacon Press, 1965.

Merton, Thomas. *Faith and Violence.* Notre Dame, Ind.: University of Notre Dame Press, 1968.

Miller, William Robert. *Nonviolence: A Christian Interpretation.* New York: Schocken Books, 1964.

Moltmann, Jürgen. *Religion, Revolution, and the Future.* Tr. M. Douglas Meeks, New York: Scribner, 1969.

Moltmann, Jürgen. *The Theology of Hope.* Tr. James W. Leitch. New York: Harper and Row, 1967.

Novack, George. *Who Will Change the World?* Toronto: YSF Publication, 1966. (pamphlet.)

Oglesby, Carl, and Richard Shaull. *Containment and Change.* New York: Macmillan, 1967.

Ramsey, Paul. *Rules and Deeds in Christian Ethics.* New York: Scribner, 1967.

Reist, Benjamin A. *Toward a Theology of Involvement: The Thought of Ernst Troeltsch.* Philadelphia: Westminster, 1966.

Rutenber, Culbert G. *The Dagger and the Cross.* New York: Fellowship Publications, 1950.

Sanders, Thomas G. *Protestant Concepts of Church and State.* Chicago: Holt, Rinehart, and Winston, 1964.

Shaull, Richard. "Revolutionary Change in Theological Perspective,"

Christian Social Ethics in a Changing World. Ed. John C. Bennett. New York: Association Press, 1966.

Sibley, Mulford Q., ed. *The Quiet Battle: Writings on the Theory and Practice of Non-violent Resistance.* Garden City, N.Y.: Anchor Books, 1963.

Sibley, Mulford. *Revolution and Violence.* Chicago: American Friends Service Committee, undated reprint from *Peace News.*

Stewart, Joffre. "Some Implications of Nonviolence in the Montgomery Resistance Movement," reprinted from *Balanced Living* (December, 1961).

Tillich, Paul. *The Protestant Era.* Chicago: University of Chicago Press, 1948.

Tillich, Paul. *Systematic Theology.* 3 vols. Chicago: University of Chicago Press, 1951-1963.

Tolstoy's Writings on Civil Disobedience and Non-Violence. New York: Bergman, 1967.

Troeltsch, Ernst. *The Social Teaching of the Christian Churches.* Tr. Olive Wyon. Vol. I-II. New York: Harper and Row, 1931.

Von Rad, Gerhard. *Old Testament Theology.* Vol. I. Tr. D. M. G. Stalker. New York: Harper and Row, 1962.

Wagner, Murray L., Jr. *In His Spirit.* Elgin, Ill.: Brethren Press, 1967.

Wagner, Murray L., Jr. "Toward a Theology of Revolution," *Brethren Life and Thought,* XI (Autumn, 1966), pp. 49-60.

Walzer, Michael. *The Revolution of the Saints.* Cambridge, Mass.: Harvard University Press, 1965.

Yoder, John Howard. *The Christian Witness to the State.* Newton, Kansas: Faith and Life Press, 1964.

Yoder, John Howard. *The Pacifism of Karl Barth.* Washington, D.C.: The Church Peace Mission, [n.d.]. (pamphlet.)

Yoder, John Howard. *Peace Without Eschatology?* Scottdale, Pa.: Mennonite Publishing House, 1954. (pamphlet.)

Yoder, John Howard. *Reinhold Niebuhr and Christian Pacifism.* Zeist, Netherlands: Heerewegen, 1954. (pamphlet.)

Yoder, John Howard. Review of Edward LeRoy Long Jr., *Conscience and Compromise, Mennonite Quarterly Review,* XXIX (January, 1955), pp. 77-80.

Zinn, Howard. *Disobedience and Democracy.* New York: Vintage Books, 1968.

Index